German
SCHOOLMATE

...ng up g...
...ase, A-Z list your Germ...
...TE tells you all about:

..sic grammatical facts with clear
explanations and useful tables

* strong or irregular verbs
* German word order and punctuation
* endings and cases
* the way German expresses important
  everyday things like days of the week,
  months, languages, numbers and dates
* German letter-writing conventions
* and much more besides

YOUR SCHOOLMATE

makes learning easier for you since it gives you
everything in one A-Z list. So if you want to
check up on the case-endings of the article, for
example, you just look up under 'der' or 'ein' in
the proper alphabetical order. Or if you want to
check whether you should invert the word order
or whether a comma is necessary you just look
up in the alphabetical list under 'word order' or
'comma'. And whenever a word is written in
CAPITAL LETTERS this means you'll find more
information under that entry. Reference is easy
– and fast.

YOUR SCHOOLMATE is ideal for:

√ language learning
√ self-study
√ exam revision
√ fast reference
√ getting things right

ab 1. As a PREPOSITION 'ab' takes the dative.
In some exceptional cases the accusative is also possible:

ab nächsten Freitag
as of next Friday

2. 'Ab' is sometimes used as an adverb, mainly in phrases without a verb (if there is a verb, the prefix **ab-** is generally used instead), or in combination with another adverb:

die nächste Straße links ab
the next road off to the left

ab morgen
from tomorrow (on)

ab und zu
now and again

ab- a SEPARABLE PREFIX used especially with verbs of motion or action with the meaning 'away' or 'off':

abfahren: der Zug fährt um 18 Uhr ab
the train leaves at 6 p.m.

abbrechen: es ist abgebrochen worden
it's been broken off

aber 1. but. 'Aber' is a CONJUNCTION that has no effect at all on the word order of the sentence.

2. 'Aber' is also used, especially in spoken German, as a 'filler' that has no particular meaning except to add emphasis:

du bist aber groß geworden!
my, how you've grown!

das ist aber nett von dir
that's very nice of you

....

accusative The accusative is used:
  1. for the direct object of the verb:
  kennst du *meinen Bruder?*
    do you know my brother?
  ich habe *dich* nicht gesehen
    I didn't see you
  2. for specifying time, distance and direction
when there is no preposition:
  er kommt mich *jeden Tag* besuchen
    he comes to see me every day
  letzten Sommer
    last summer
  nächsten Freitag
    next Friday
  ich gehe *keinen Schritt* weiter
    I won't go a step further
  **es liegt nur *einen Kilometer* südlich von
    hier** it's only one kilometre to the south
  3. in phrases which tell you more about the
manner of a person or action (this construction
tends to be literary German):
  **er kam herein, *den Rucksack* noch auf
    dem Rücken** he came in with his rucksack
    still on his back
  4. after certain PREPOSITIONS.
  5. with certain adjectives:
    gewohnt   *used to*
    los   *rid of*
    müde*   *tired of*
    satt   *fed up with*
    voll*   *full of*
    wert*   *worth*
*see also GENITIVE; 'müde' only takes the
accusative in the construction 'ich bin es müde'
(*I'm tired of it*).
  6. in certain idioms, for example:
  vielen Dank!
    thank you very much
  guten Morgen/Tag/Abend!

addresses When addressing an envelope, the name of the person to whom you are writing should always be in the accusative. This is particularly important to remember as 'Herr' is a weak noun and adds -**n** in the accusative.

On the line following the name of the person comes the street name with the house number after it. 'Straße' is frequently abbreviated to 'Str.', and is quite often added to the actual name of the street as part of the same word.

The next line starts with the area code of the town ('die Postleitzahl') followed by the name of the town. Sometimes the international country code (which is the same as that used on cars) is put before the area code instead of writing the country at the bottom of the address.

> Herrn
> D. Wachendorf
> Maximilianstr. 20
> A-6020 Innsbruck

On the reverse side of the envelope, or in the top lefthand corner of the front, it is customary to put your own address, sometimes with 'Absender:' or 'Abs.:' before it.

adjectives ◆I *Declension*

Adjectives can be used in two ways. If they are used predicatively, that is after a verb, they are not declined. If they are used attributively, that is in front of a noun, then they are declined. There are three different sets of declensional endings; which one is used depends on which article, if any, comes before the adjective.

1. Weak endings

	masc	*sing* *fem*	*neut*	*pl* *all genders*
nom	-e	-e	-e	-en
acc	-en	-e	-e	-en
gen	-en	-en	-en	-en
dat	-en	-en	-en	-en

The weak endings are used after:

der	jeder
dieser	mancher (*sing*), manche (*pl*)*
jener	alle (*pl*)
welcher	solcher

*can also be followed by the strong endings.

2. Strong endings

	sing			pl
	masc	fem	neut	all genders
nom	-er	-e	-es	-e
acc	-en	-e	-es	-e
gen	-en	-er	-en	-er
dat	-em	-er	-em	-en

The strong endings are used if an adjective stands alone before a noun, or comes after a number, or comes after:

ein paar	manche*
einige	viele
mehrere (*pl*)	wenige

*can also be followed by the weak endings.

3. Mixed endings

	sing			pl
	masc	fem	neut	all genders
nom	-er	-e	-es	-en
acc	-en	-e	-es	-en
gen	-en	-en	-en	-en
dat	-en	-en	-en	-en

The mixed endings are used after:

ein	dein	unser
kein	sein	euer
mein	ihr	Ihr/ihr

If two adjectives stand together before a noun, the general rule is that both have the same endings. If however there is no article in front of them, and they are in the dative masculine or neuter singular, then the second one may have -en instead of -em as its ending:

mit großem, unerwartetem (or unerwarteten) Erfolg
   with great and unexpected success

There are a few cases where the stem of an adjective changes when an ending is added, in that an unstressed **-e-** is dropped. It is always dropped in adjectives ending in **-el**; usually dropped in those ending in **-er** after two vowels; and can be dropped in those which end in **-er** or **-en**:

dunkel: ein dunkles Zimmer
a dark room
sauer: saure Gurken
pickled gherkins
hager: ein hageres (*or* **hagres**) **Gesicht**
a gaunt face

◆II *Use as Nouns*

Many adjectives can be used as nouns. They are written with a capital letter but they have exactly the same endings as they do when they are used as adjectives. Their grammatical gender corresponds to their real-life gender – masculine for men, feminine for women, and neuter for things and qualities.

der Alte, der nebenan wohnt
the old man who lives next door
die Alte, die mir gegenüber saß
the old lady who was sitting opposite me
das Komische daran
the funny thing about it

Adjectives are also used as nouns after 'etwas', 'viel', 'wenig', 'nichts', 'allerlei' and 'alles'. After 'alles' they have the weak neuter endings; after all the others the strong neuter endings:

alles Gute!
all the best!
er hat ja nichts Neues gesagt
he didn't say anything new

adverbs A great many adverbs have the same form as the predicative adjective:
er hat sich ganz *schlimm* verletzt
he's hurt himself quite badly

....

sie spricht immer sehr *leise*
> she always talks very quietly

Sometimes the ending '-erweise' is added; this shows that the adverb is being used to comment on the whole sentence rather than just describing the manner in which the verb is carried out:

komischerweise wollte sie nicht
> funnily enough, she didn't want to

age Here are some useful phrases connected with age:

wie alt sind Sie?
> how old are you?

ich bin achtzehn (Jahre alt)
> I'm eighteen (years old *or* years of age)

mit fünf (Jahren) bin ich in die Schule gekommen
> I started school when I was five (years old)

als ich in deinem Alter war
> when I was your age

wenn du in mein Alter kommst
> when you get to (*or* are) my age

wann sind Sie geboren?
> when were you born?

ich bin (*or* wurde) 1963 geboren
> I was born in 1963

aller, alle, alles can be used as an adjective, meaning 'all, every', or as a pronoun, meaning 'everyone, everything, all (of them)'. The declension is the same for both.

	masc	*sing* *fem*	*neut*	*pl* *all genders*
nom	aller	alle	alles	alle
acc	allen	alle	alles	alle
gen	allen (+s)	aller	allen (+s)	aller
dat	allem	aller	allem	allen

adj: **alle Bücher**
> all the books

trotz aller Mühe
> in spite of all the effort

pronoun: **alles, was er sagt**
> everything he says

sie sind alle so alt
> they are all so old

das ist mir alles gleich
> it's all the same to me

alles in allem
> all in all

When 'aller, alle, alles' is used as an adjective, any other adjective coming between it and the noun has the weak ADJECTIVE endings:

alle ausländischen Studenten
> all foreign students

When 'alles' is used as a pronoun, an adjective coming after it has the weak endings and is, with only one or two exceptions, written with a capital letter:

dann wünsche ich dir alles Gute
> well then, all the best to you

sie hat alles Mögliche getan
> she did everything possible

but: **sie hat alles mögliche mitgebracht**
> she brought all sorts of things

alles übrige
> everything else

There is also an uninflected form **'all'** which is used before 'der, die, das', 'dieser, diese, dieses', 'jener, jene, jenes', and the possessives 'mein, meine, mein' etc:

all mein Zureden
> all my persuasion

wegen all der Probleme
> because of all the problems

But in the feminine and the plural nominative and accusative it is also possible to use the form 'alle':

all(e) meine Mühe
> all my efforts

all(e) diese Gedichte
> all these poems

....

alphabet The German alphabet is
pronounced as follows:
 a [ah] **b** [bay] **c** [tsay] **d** [day] **e** [ay] **f** [eff] **g** [gay]
 h [hah] **i** [ee] **j** [yot] **k** [kah] **l** [el] **m** [em] **n** [en]
 o [oh] **p** [pay] **q** [koo] **r** [air] **s** [ess] **t** [tay] **u** [oo]
 v [fow] **w** [vay] **x** [iks] **y** [oop-see-lon] **z** [tset]

als is used in two main ways – as a
CONJUNCTION meaning WHEN, and to make
COMPARISONS.
  Als ob and **als wenn** are used to mean 'as if, as
though'. There is no difference in meaning
between them. The verb following either of them
is in the SUBJUNCTIVE:
    als ob ich das nicht wüßte
       as if I didn't know that
  Instead of 'als ob' and 'als wenn' it is also
possible to use 'als' by itself (again with the
SUBJUNCTIVE):
    er benahm sich, als wäre er ...
       he behaved as though he were ...
  See also EIN (I 3).

am is a one-word contraction of 'an dem'. It
usually replaces the full form except where 'dem'
means 'that particular ...'. It is always used
instead of the full form in place names, in dates,
and in forming the superlative of predicative
adjectives and adverbs:
    Frankfurt am Main
       Frankfurt (on the Main)
    am 2. Mai
       on the second of May
    am Freitagabend
       on Friday evening
    das wäre am besten
       that would be the best thing
    sie saß am Tisch
       she was sitting at the table
  but: **sie saß gerade an dem Tisch, wo ...**
       she was sitting at that very table where ...

an takes either the accusative or the dative, depending on whether it is expressing movement or not. See PREPOSITIONS.

an- a SEPARABLE PREFIX.

and(e)rer, and(e)re, and(e)res can be used either as an adjective, in which case it takes the ordinary weak, strong, or mixed adjective endings as appropriate (see section I of the entry ADJECTIVES), or as a pronoun, when it takes the strong adjective endings.

The **-e-** in the stem is always optional and often left out. A further variation is possible with 'anderen' and 'anderem', in that if the **-e-** of the stem is kept, the **-e-** of the ending can be left out.

adj: **ein anderes** *or* **andres Buch**
      another book, a different book
  alle anderen *or* **andren** *or* **andern Männer**
      all other men
pronoun: **habt ihr die anderen** *or* **andren** *or*
      andern getroffen? did you meet the others?

anders is an adverb; unlike 'and(e)rer, and(e)re, and(e)res', it never changes its form:
  jemand/niemand/irgendwo anders
      somebody/nobody/somewhere else
  ich hatte es mir anders vorgestellt
      I had imagined it differently
  es geht nicht anders
      there's no other way

ans is a one-word contraction of 'an das'. It usually replaces the full form except where 'das' means 'that particular ...'. See AM for example.

articles see DER, DIE, DAS and EIN.

attributive An adjective is used attributively when it comes in front of its noun.

auf takes either the accusative or the dative, depending on whether it is expressing movement or not. See PREPOSITIONS.

auf- a SEPARABLE PREFIX, the main meanings of
which are 'up', 'on', and 'open':
>**aufblicken: sie blickte auf** she looked up
>**aufsteigen: Günter stieg auf sein Fahrrad
>auf** Günter got onto his bicycle
>**auflassen: laß doch das Fenster auf!**
>leave the window open!

aufs is a one-word contraction of 'auf das'. It
usually replaces the full form except where 'das'
means 'that particular ...'. See AM for example.

aus takes the dative. See PREPOSITIONS.

aus- a SEPARABLE PREFIX used mainly with the
meaning 'out':
>**ausgehen: wollen wir heute abend
>ausgehen?** shall we go out this evening?
>**auspacken: ich habe meine Sachen noch
>nicht ausgepackt** I haven't unpacked my
>things yet

außer takes the dative. See PREPOSITIONS.

außerhalb takes the genitive. See
PREPOSITIONS.

auxiliary verbs are used with either the
past participle or the infinitive of another verb in
order to form certain tenses of that second verb.
The three auxiliaries are HABEN, SEIN, WERDEN.
  1. 'Haben' is used with the past participle to
form the perfect and pluperfect tenses of:
>—all transitive verbs;
>—all REFLEXIVE verbs;
>—all MODAL verbs;
>—all intransitive verbs which do not describe a
change of place or state, except 'bleiben', 'sein',
'geschehen', and 'gelingen':
>**ich habe sie nicht gesehen**
>I didn't see her
>**hat er sich schon gemeldet?**
>has he been in touch yet?

sie hatte die Platte hören wollen
she had wanted to hear the record
du hast nicht lange darüber nachgedacht
you didn't think about it for very long
2. 'Sein' is used with the past participle to form
the perfect and pluperfect tenses of:
—all intransitive verbs which do describe a
change of place or state;
—'bleiben' (=*stay*), 'sein' (=*be*), 'geschèhen'
(=*happen*), and 'gelingen' (=*succeed*):
warum seid ihr nicht gekommen?
why didn't you come?
**der Rhein ist letzten Winter zweimal
zugefroren** the Rhine froze over twice last
winter
ich war gerade eingeschlafen
I had just gone to sleep
wieso ist sie so lange weggeblieben?
why has she stayed away so long?
3. 'Werden' is used with the infinitive to form
the future and conditional tenses of all verbs:
das werde ich auf keinen Fall tun!
there's no way I'm going to do that
das würde ich nicht sagen
I wouldn't say that
It is also used with the past participle to form
the PASSIVE:
das wird nicht erwähnt
that isn't mentioned
er wurde erschossen he was shot (dead)

-bar is an adjective suffix meaning '-able'. It is
usually added to the stem of a verb:
diese Krankheit ist heilbar
this disease is curable (*or* can be cured)

be- an INSEPARABLE PREFIX. It can make the
verb to which it is attached transitive:
wohnen to live – **bewohnen** to live in
gucken to look – **begucken** to look at

bei takes the dative. See PREPOSITIONS.

....

beide can be used both as an adjective and as a pronoun. If it is used as an adjective standing on its own before a noun, or if it is used after a personal pronoun, it has the strong adjective endings (see section I of the entry ADJECTIVES):

beide Mädchen both (the) girls
wir beide both of us

If it is used after 'der, die, das', 'dieser, diese, dieses', 'jener, jene, jenes', 'alle', or a possessive adjective, it has the weak adjective endings:

die beiden Mädchen the two girls
diese beiden Zimmer these two rooms

When it is used as a pronoun, it always has the strong adjective endings:

alle beide wollten mitkommen
    both of them wanted to come

There is also a neuter singular form of the pronoun, **beides**, which may be used to refer to things, ideas, etc, but not to people:

beides ist möglich both are possible

beim is a one-word contraction of 'bei dem'. It usually replaces the full form except where 'dem' means 'that particular ...'. See AM for example.

bis takes the accusative. See PREPOSITIONS.

capital letters are used at the beginning of sentences in German in the same way as they are in English. But they are also used in situations where English would use a small letter:

1. All German nouns are written with a capital.
2. Adjectives which are used as nouns after the definite article, 'etwas', 'viel', 'wenig', 'nichts', 'allerlei' and 'alles' are generally written with a capital:

das Gute/das Schöne
    the good, goodness/the beautiful, beauty
etwas Schönes something beautiful
nichts Neues nothing new
but: **das andere, etwas anderes**
    the other, something else

3. Verb infinitives which are used as nouns are written with a capital:
    etwas zum Lesen
      something to read
    das Summen
      the buzzing
4. The polite form of 'you', 'your', etc, is always written with a capital:
    könnten Sie mir vielleicht sagen, ...?
      could you please tell me ...?
5. The familiar forms of 'you', 'your', etc, are always given a capital in LETTER-WRITING.

cases See NOMINATIVE, ACCUSATIVE, GENITIVE, and DATIVE.

-chen See DIMINUTIVES.

collective nouns are singular in German:
    das Vieh brüllte
      the cattle were mooing
    warten Sie, bis die Polizei kommt
      wait until the police arrive

colons have one use in German which they do not have consistently in English, and that is to introduce direct speech:
    dann sagte sie: „Das mache ich nicht!"
      then she said, 'I won't do that!'
A colon is only used if the verb which reports the direct speech comes before what is quoted; if the verb comes in the middle or after what is quoted, then a comma is used as in English.

commas are used between a series of nouns or adjectives in German in much the same way as they are in English, but unlike English there are quite strict rules about where commas should be used between clauses:
1. All subordinate clauses should be separated off by commas:
    mach das Licht an, wenn es zu dunkel wird put the light on if it gets too dark

mein Bruder, der verheiratet ist, hat es mir gegeben my brother, who's married, gave it to me

ich glaube nicht, daß er noch ankommt, bevor du abfährst I don't think he'll arrive before you leave

The only exception is when two or more subordinate clauses are linked by 'und' or 'oder'. In this case they are not separated from each other if they both have the same subject, but they should still be separated off from the main clause by a comma:

ich weiß, daß du viel zu tun hast und daß du deshalb nicht kommst, aber ... I know you've a lot to do and so you won't be coming, but ...

2. Main clauses should be separated by a comma if they are not linked by 'und' or 'oder':

es war nicht kalt, aber es war auch nicht richtig warm it wasn't cold, but it wasn't really warm either

3. Main clauses linked with 'und' or 'oder' should be separated by a comma unless they are very short or share the same subject:

es wurde immer kälter, und wir wollten nach Hause it was getting colder all the time and we wanted to go home

but:

sie stiegen in den Wagen ein und fuhren los they got into the car and drove off

4. Generally the infinitive with 'zu' is not separated from the rest of the sentence:

sie fing an zu lesen she began to read

But if the infinitive phrase is expanded in any way, a comma should be used:

sie fing an, den Brief zu lesen she started to read the letter

sie fing an, schneller zu lesen she started to read faster

5. In German the comma replaces the full stop
for decimals:

3,33 *(spoken: 'drei Komma dreiunddreißig)*
3.33.

comparison ◆I *Comparison of adjectives*

The comparative of most adjectives is formed by
adding **-er**.

The superlative of most adjectives is formed by
using **der/die/das ...-ste**. The predicative
superlative is also formed by using **am ...sten**:

sie ist die Schönste *or* **sie ist am schönsten**
she is the most beautiful

Adjectives ending in **-el**, **-auer** and **-euer**
always drop the **-e-** in the comparative, and
adjectives ending in **-en** or **-er** may optionally
drop it. Adjectives ending in **-d**, **-s**, **-sch**, **-ß**, **-t** or **-z**
add an **-e-** before the superlative ending if they
have only one syllable or if the last syllable is
stressed. Adjectives ending in **-haft** or **-los** always
add this **-e-** regardless of stress.

neu	*new*	neuer	am neuesten
dunkel	*dark*	dunkler	am dunkelsten
teuer	*dear*	teurer	am teuersten
trocken	*dry*	trock(e)ner	am trockensten
heiß	*hot*	heißer	am heißesten
rasch	*fast*	rascher	am raschesten
öd	*bleak*	öder	am ödesten

A number of adjectives of one syllable whose
vowel is **a**, **o** or **u** add an umlaut in both the
comparative and the superlative. In a few cases
the umlaut is optional, but with the following
adjectives it is obligatory:

alt	*old*	älter	am ältesten
arg	*terrible*	ärger	am ärgsten
arm	*poor*	ärmer	am ärmsten
grob	*coarse*	gröber	am gröbsten
hart	*hard*	härter	am härtesten
jung	*young*	jünger	am jüngsten
kalt	*cold*	kälter	am kältesten

klug	clever	klüger	am klügsten
krank	ill	kränker	am kränksten
kurz	short	kürzer	am kürzesten
lang	long	länger	am längsten
scharf	sharp	schärfer	am schärfsten
schwach	weak	schwächer	am schwächsten

The following adjectives are irregular:

groß	big	größer	am größten
gut	good	besser	am besten
hoch	high	höher	am höchsten
nah	near	näher	am nächsten
viel	many	mehr	am meisten

◆II *Comparison of adverbs*

Adverbs form their comparative and superlative in the same way as predicative adjectives:

ich lief schneller als er

I ran faster than he did

sein Bruder lief am schnellsten

his brother ran (the) fastest (of all)

The following adverbs are irregular in their comparison, or have alternative forms:

bald	soon	eher	am ehesten
		früher	am frühesten
gern	willingly	lieber	am liebsten
gut,			
wohl	well	besser	am besten
oft	often	öfter	am häufigsten
			am öftesten
viel,	very		
sehr	(much)	mehr	am meisten
wenig	little	weniger.	am wenigsten
		minder	

The German superlative can also be used in some constructions to mean 'extremely ...':

sie war aufs tiefste beleidigt

she was very deeply offended

◆III *General comparisons*

If you want to say 'as ... as' or 'as', the German structure is **so ... wie** or **so**:

Franz fährt so schnell wie Karl
Franz drives as fast as Karl
doppelt/halb so teuer
twice/half as expensive
If you want to say 'more than' or '-er ... than' the
German structure is **-er als**:
Franz fährt schneller als Karl
Franz drives faster than Karl
**er hat sich besser verhalten, als wir
erwartet hatten** he behaved better than
we had expected

compounds in German are made up of two
or more words. They need not necessarily be
nouns, but the vast majority are. The gender of a
compound is always the same as the gender of the
last word in it. Most noun compounds are made up
of a noun plus another noun, but these can be
linked in various ways. There are no hard and fast
rules to tell you how any two nouns should be
linked, but there are general tendencies.
  1. Noun + Noun, without any linking letters –
used especially when the first word of the
compound is a monosyllable or ends in a vowel:
     das Festessen *banquet*
     der Autofahrer *motorist*
  2. Noun + e + Noun – used more in established
words rather than in newly-formed compounds:
     das Mauseloch *mousehole*
  3. Noun + (e)n + Noun – used especially when
the first word of the compound is a feminine noun
or a weak masculine noun:
     der Sonnenschein *sunshine*
     der Studentenausweis *student card*
  4. Noun + er + Noun – used especially when the
plural form of the first noun ends in **-er** and it
makes sense in the compound if that noun is
plural:
     die Götterdämmerung *twilight of the gods*
     der Kinderspielplatz *children's
                            playground*

5. Noun + s + Noun – used when the first noun
ends in **-heit**, **-ing**, **-ion**, **-keit**, **-ling**, **-schaft**, **-tät**,
-tum, or **-ung**, or is a verb infinitive used as a
noun:

    die Qualitätsarbeit   *quality work*
    der Regierungschef   *head of government*

6. Noun + es + Noun – used especially when the
first noun is masculine or neuter and only one
syllable long, and it makes sense for the first noun
to be in the genitive singular:

    der Gottessohn   *Son of God*
    der Geisteszustand   *mental state*

7. Verb infinitive minus -en + Noun:

    die Waschmaschine   *washing machine*
    das Rasierapparat   *shaver*

conditional tense   This corresponds in
English to either 'I would (*or* should) come', or 'I
would (*or* should) be coming'.

The conditional tense can also be expressed by
using the imperfect SUBJUNCTIVE:

    ich würde mitgehen, wenn ich Zeit hätte
      or **ich ginge mit, wenn ich Zeit hätte**
      I would go too if I had time

See the entry VERBS.

conditional perfect tense   This
corresponds in English to either 'I would (*or*
should) have sung', or 'I would (*or* should) have
been singing':

    wenn alles geklappt hätte, würdest du im
        Chor gesungen haben
      if everything had worked out you would
        have sung (*or* would have been singing)
        in the choir

As the conditional perfect is rather clumsy in
German, the pluperfect SUBJUNCTIVE is often used
instead:

    ich hätte sonst gesungen
      I would have sung otherwise

See the entry VERBS.

conjunctions   fall into two groups,
according to whether or not they affect the WORD
ORDER.

1. Co-ordinating conjunctions have absolutely
no effect on the word order. There is only a small
group of them:

aber	*but*
beziehungsweise	*or*
denn	*because, for*
doch	*but*
jedoch	*however*
oder	*or*
sondern	*but, on the contrary*
und	*and*

They can be used to connect nouns, adjectives,
or clauses; when they connect clauses, all of them
except 'und' and 'oder' always require a COMMA
between the two clauses.

2. Subordinating conjunctions affect the word
order; they introduce subordinate clauses and so
they send the verb to the end of the clause. There
should always be a comma between the two
clauses:

als	*when, as, than*
als ob	*as if*
als wenn	*as if*
(an)statt daß	*instead of ...ing*
bevor	*before*
bis	*until, by*
da	*since, as*
damit	*so that, in order that*
daß	*that, so that*
ehe	*before*
falls	*in case, if*
indem	*while, as*
nachdem	*after*
ob	*whether, if*
obgleich	*although*
obschon	*although*
obwohl	*although*

....

seit(dem)	*since*
sobald	*as soon as*
so daß	*with the result that*
solange	*as long as*
sooft	*as often as*
sowie	*as soon as*
während	*while*
weil	*because*
wenn	*if, when(ever)*
wie	*as*

The INTERROGATIVE WORDS are also used as subordinating conjunctions.

countries Most countries are talked about without an article in German; theoretically they are neuter, but the gender is only apparent when an adjective is used with the name of the country. There are a few exceptions which are not neuter and which are always preceded by 'der' or 'die':

1. Masculine

der Libanon	*Lebanon*
der Sudan	*(the) Sudan*

2. Feminine

die Bundesrepublik	*West Germany*
die DDR	*the GDR*
die Schweiz	*Switzerland*
die Sowjetunion	*the Soviet Union*
die UdSSR	*the USSR*
die Tschechoslowakei	*Czechoslovakia*
die Türkei	*Turkey*

3. Plural

die Niederlande	*the Netherlands*
die USA	*the USA*
die Vereinigten Staaten	*the United States*

In most cases, 'to (a country)' is translated by **nach**. But if the country is one of those which is always used with 'der' or 'die', **in** plus the accusative is used instead:

wir fahren nach Deutschland/in die Schweiz we're going to Germany/ Switzerland

da 1. as, because. 'Da' is a CONJUNCTION that affects the word order of the sentence.

2. there. As an adverb of place, 'da' is only used with verbs of position; with verbs of movement, DAHIN- and DAHER- are used instead.

3. 'Da' is occasionally used as a RELATIVE PRONOUN meaning 'when', but only in literary language.

da- 1. a SEPARABLE PREFIX used with verbs that express position, with the meaning 'there':
> **dableiben: sie ist noch eine Weile dageblieben** she stayed on there a while longer

2. 'da-' (or 'dar-' before vowels) often combines with prepositions to form a single word meaning 'to/from/above *etc* it'. See PERSONAL PRONOUNS.

3. 'da-' (or 'dar-') also combines with SEPARABLE PREFIXES. When this happens, 'da-' and the prefix can be separated from the verb but never from each other:
> **davonlaufen: seine Frau ist ihm davongelaufen** his wife has walked out on him

daher- a SEPARABLE PREFIX used mainly with verbs expressing movement from a place, with the meaning 'along' or 'up to the speaker':
> **daherkommen: dann ist auch noch ihr Bruder dahergekommen** then her brother came along too

dahin- a SEPARABLE PREFIX used with verbs of movement meaning 'past or away from the speaker', and with some other verbs with the meaning 'without thinking very much':
> **dahinfliegen: eine Lerche flog dahin** a lark flew past
> **dahinsagen: das habe ich nur so dahingesagt** I just said that without thinking

dann   then. 'Dann' is sometimes used in the construction **wenn ..., dann ...**:

> **wenn das stimmt, dann müßte ich mich bei ihm entschuldigen** if that's true (then) I should apologize to him

dar-   1. See DA-.

2. A SEPARABLE PREFIX used with verbs to give the meaning of public or explicit presentation of something:

> **darlegen: im nächsten Kapitel legt er seine eigenen Theorien dar** in the next chapter he expounds his own theories

das   nominative and accusative neuter singular of the definite article and the pronoun DER, DIE, DAS.

daß   that, so that. 'Daß' is a CONJUNCTION that affects the word order of the sentence.

dates   The days of the week, the months of the year, and the four seasons are all masculine and are generally used with 'der' (or 'den', 'des', or 'dem' according to the case).

When the day of the month is said or written, 'der' is used before the number; the month comes after the number:

> **heute ist der 6. (***spoken*** sechste) April, heute haben wir den 6. (***spoken*** sechsten) April** it's the sixth of April today

> **der Wievielte ist heute?, den Wievielten haben wir heute?** what's the date today?

> **am 2. (***spoken*** zweiten) Mai** on the second of May

> **am Mittwoch, dem 8. (***spoken*** achten) Juli** on Wednesday, July the eighth

When a date consists simply of a year, it is given either without any preposition at all or after the phrase 'im Jahre'. The '... hundert...' is never omitted when the figures are read out:

im Jahre 1983 (*pronounced:*
    neunzehnhundertdreiundachtzig) in 1983
er wurde 1921 geboren
    he was born in 1921
1933 war Deutschland noch ...
    in 1933 Germany was still ...
At the top of letters many people give the date
completely in figures, but when it is written out in
full the accusative case is always used:
Hamburg, den 16.7.81
Hamburg, den 16. Juli 1981

dative The dative is used:
1. for the indirect object of the verb:
    sie zeigte *meiner Mutter* den Brief
        she showed the letter to my mother
    wer hat *dir* denn das gesagt?
        who told you that?
2. meaning 'for someone, on someone's behalf':
    sie hat *mir* den Koffer getragen
        she carried my case for me
3. instead of a possessive adjective with parts of
the body, items of clothing and 'das Leben':
    ich muß *mir* die Hände waschen
        I must wash my hands
    sie hat *ihm* das Leben gerettet
        she saved his life
    ich habe *mir* die Hose zerrissen
        I've torn my trousers
But note:
    wasch dir dein dreckiges Gesicht
        wash your filthy face
4. after certain PREPOSITIONS.
5. instead of the accusative case with certain
verbs:

ähneln	*resemble*	entkommen	*escape from*
antworten	*answer*	fehlen	*
begegnen	*meet*	folgen	*follow*
danken	*thank*	gefallen	*please*
dienen	*serve*	gehorchen	*obey*
drohen	*threaten*	gehören	*belong to*

gelingen	*	passen	suit
gelten	be aimed at	schaden	harm
genügen	be enough for	schmecken	*
gleichen	be like	schmeicheln	flatter
gratulieren	congratulate	trauen	trust
helfen	help	trotzen	defy
mißfallen	displease	vertrauen	trust
mißtrauen	distrust	widersprechen	contradict
nachlaufen	run after	zuhören	listen to
nahen	approach	zusehen	watch

*du fehlst mir sehr
I miss you a lot

ist es ihm gelungen?
was he successful?

wie schmeckt dir der Kuchen?
how do you like the cake?

6. with certain adjectives:

ähnlich	similar (to)
behilflich	helpful (to)
bekannt	known (to)
dankbar	grateful (to)
eigen	peculiar (to)
gehorsam	obedient (to)
gleich	the same (as)
langweilig	boring (for)
nützlich	useful (to)
schädlich	harmful (to)
unbekannt	unknown (to)

7. in certain idioms, for example:

ist dir kalt?
are you cold?

mir ist schlecht
I'm feeling ill

du bist mir vielleicht einer!
you're a right one, you are!

das ist mir zu teuer
that's too expensive (for me)

es ist mir völlig egal
it's all the same to me

Nouns whose plural form does not already end in -n, add -n in the dative plural.

In the singular, masculine and neuter nouns which do not end in **-en, -em, -el, -er, -ling**, or a vowel, can optionally add **-e** in the dative, or **-se** if they end in **-nis**.

days of the week are masculine.

Sonntag	Donnerstag
Montag	Freitag
Dienstag	Samstag (*in S. Germany*) *or*
Mittwoch	Sonnabend (*in N. and East Germany*)

A particular day is generally referred to either in the accusative case without an article, or in the dative with the preposition 'an' and an article:

wir sehen uns (am) Dienstag wieder
   we'll meet again on Tuesday
wir fahren erst am Freitag weiter
   we're not going on until Friday
am ersten Mittwoch im September
   on the first Wednesday in September

If something happens regularly on the same day of the week, **-s** is added to the name of the day, which then has a small letter:

dienstags gehe ich schwimmen
   I go swimming on Tuesdays

Here are some other useful phrases:

Sonntag morgen/nachmittag/abend
   Sunday morning/afternoon/evening
in der Nacht auf Freitag (*or* **von Donnerstag auf Freitag**)
   during Thursday night
jeden Dienstag every Tuesday
eines Mittwochs one Wednesday
Sonnabend in einer Woche (*or* **in acht Tagen**) a week on Saturday
Montag vor einer Woche (*or* **vor acht Tagen**) a week ago on Monday
am Donnerstag, den 14. April
   on Thursday, April 14th

declensions see NOUNS and ADJECTIVES.

....

definite article see DER, DIE, DAS.

dein your (*sing*). See POSSESSIVES.

demonstratives The main demonstratives
are:

DER, die, das, (*pl*) die
DIESER, diese, dieses, (*pl*) diese
JENER, jene, jenes, (*pl*) jene
DERJENIGE, diejenige, dasjenige, (*pl*) diejenigen
DERSELBE, dieselbe, dasselbe, (*pl*) dieselben
DERARTIGER, derartige, derartiges, (*pl*)
    derartige
SOLCHER, solche, solches, (*pl*) solche

denn 1. because, for. 'Denn' is a CONJUNCTION
which has no effect on the word order of the clause
it introduces, but it must have a comma before it:
wir blieben zu Hause, denn es regnete
    we stayed at home because it was raining
2. than, especially in the phrase 'denn je':
häufiger/schöner denn je
    more frequently/more beautiful than ever
3. **es sei denn, …** unless …
4. 'denn' can also be used for general emphasis,
especially in questions:
was ist denn hier los? what's going on here?
warum denn nicht? why (ever) not?
wo bleibt er denn? where has he/it got to?

der, die, das has three functions in German.
It is of course the definite article, but it can also be
a pronoun, either in a main clause or introducing
a subordinate (relative) clause. It has slightly
different forms for each function.

◆I *The definite article*

| | sing | | | pl |
	masc	fem	neut	all genders
nom	der	die	das	die
acc	den	die	das	die
gen	des(+s)	der	des(+s)	der
dat	dem	der	dem	den(+n)

Remen.ber to add the genitive singular ending (usually **-s** or **-es**) to masculine and neuter nouns, and the dative plural ending **-n** to all nouns whose plural does not already end in **-n**.

The definite article is used:

1. to translate 'the';

2. with proper nouns when they are used with an adjective:

die kleine Helga
    little Helga

das heutige Deutschland
    present-day Germany

3. with the names of people, when you are speaking or writing quite informally:

da ist ja der Peter!
    there's Peter!

kommt die Ulrike auch mit?
    is Ulrike coming too?

4. with the names of rivers, lakes and mountains:

der Rhein   the Rhine
die Themse   the (river) Thames
der Bodensee Lake Constance
der Ätna   Mount Etna

5. with the names of streets, squares and churches:

ich wohne in der Bahnhofstraße
    I live in Bahnhofstraße

die Josefskirche ist am Wilhelmsplatz
    St Joseph's (Church) is in Wilhelmsplatz

6. with the names of COUNTRIES which are feminine or plural:

die Schweiz   Switzerland
in den Vereinigten   in the USA
    Staaten

7. instead of a possessive adjective with parts of the body, items of clothing, and 'das Leben', when they do not have a descriptive adjective in front of them:

nimm die Hände aus der Tasche!
    take your hands out of your pockets!

....

ich muß mir die Haare schneiden lassen
I must get my hair cut

See also DATIVE 3.

8. with nouns connected with time, such as the days of the week, the time of day, meals, and seasons:

am Mittwoch	on Wednesday
nach dem Frühstück	after breakfast
der Frühling kommt	spring is coming

9. in such expressions as:

2 Mark das Kilo	2 marks a kilo
50 Pfennig das Stück	50 pfennigs each
zweimal im Monat	twice a month

10. with infinitives used as nouns:

ihm fiel das Atmen schwer
he found it hard to breathe

du solltest dir das Rauchen abgewöhnen
you ought to give up smoking

11. with a great many abstract nouns:

die Liebe	love
die Gesellschaft	society
der Durst	thirst

12. in certain idiomatic expressions:

in die Kirche	to church
in der Schule	at school
im Bett	in bed
mit dem Bus/Zug	by bus/train

◆ II *Pronoun in a main clause (demonstrative)*

	sing			pl
	masc	*fem*	*neut*	*all genders*
nom	der	die	das	die
acc	den	die	das	die
gen	dessen	deren	dessen	deren/derer
dat	dem	der	dem	denen

When 'der, die, das' is used as a demonstrative pronoun it has the general meaning 'this man/woman/thing':

wer hat dir das gesagt?
who told you that?

deine Schwester? die kenne ich nicht
 your sister? I don't know her
ich bin mir dessen bewußt
 I'm aware of that
The genitive plural is usually 'deren', but when there is a subordinate clause beginning with a relative pronoun (who, which etc) after it, the form 'derer' is used:

er war früher mal mit ihnen befreundet, aber jetzt erinnert er sich *deren* nicht mehr he was once very friendly with them, but now he doesn't remember them any more
er erinnert sich *derer* nicht mehr, mit denen er früher mal befreundet war he now no longer remembers the people he was once very friendly with

◆ III *Pronoun introducing a subordinate clause (relative)*

	masc	*fem*	*neut*	*all genders*
		sing		*pl*
nom	der	die	das	die
acc	den	die	das	die
gen	dessen	deren	dessen	deren
dat	dem	der	dem	denen

See also RELATIVE PRONOUNS.

derartig is used as an adjective and takes the ordinary weak, strong, or mixed adjective endings as appropriate (see section I of ADJECTIVES):

sie ist mit einer derartigen Geschwindigkeit gefahren, daß ... she drove so fast that ...
derartige Pläne schlagen fast immer fehl plans like that nearly always go wrong
When 'derartig' is followed by a second adjective then the word 'derartig' itself is not normally declined:
(ein) derartig schlechtes Wetter such terrible weather

deren genitive feminine singular and genitive plural of the pronoun DER, DIE, DAS.

derer genitive plural of the demonstrative pronoun DER, DIE, DAS.

derjenige declines in exactly the same way as DERSELBE. It can be used either as an article (that is, instead of 'a' or 'the' before a noun), or as a pronoun, with the meaning 'the man/woman/... who'. But in both cases there is always a relative clause separated off by commas further on in the sentence, and any adjective coming immediately after 'derjenige' always has the weak ADJECTIVE endings:

> **diejenigen Bücher, die ich gelesen habe**
> the books that I've read
> **diejenigen, die ich nicht mehr brauche**
> the ones that I don't need any longer

derselbe was originally two words – an article and an adjective – and although they are always written as one word nowadays, both parts still decline.

	masc	sing fem	neut	pl all genders
nom	derselbe	dieselbe	dasselbe	dieselben
acc	denselben	dieselbe	dasselbe	dieselben
gen	desselben	derselben	desselben	derselben
dat	demselben	derselben	demselben	denselben

'Derselbe' can be used either as an article (that is, instead of 'a' or 'the' before a noun), or as a pronoun, with the meaning 'the same man/woman/...'. In both cases any adjective coming immediately after it has the weak ADJECTIVE endings, and any comparison following it uses **wie**:

> **wir haben denselben Namen**
> we have the same name
> **ich gehe zu demselben Arzt wie ihre Schwester** I go to the same doctor as her sister

er sagt jedesmal dasselbe
  he says the same thing every time
sie war nicht mehr dieselbe
  she was no longer the same person

dessen masculine and neuter genitive
singular of the pronoun DER, DIE, DAS:
  der Mann, dessen Frau ...
    the man whose wife ...
  der Wagen, dessen Karosserie ... or (*more
    commonly*) **der Wagen, von dem die
    Karosserie ...** the car whose bodywork ...

desto See JE.

deutsch See LANGUAGES.

dich accusative of 'du'. See PERSONAL
PRONOUNS.

die feminine nominative and accusative
singular, and nominative and accusative plural of
the definite article and the pronoun DER, DIE, DAS.

dieser, diese, dieses can be used either as
an article (that is, instead of 'a' or 'the' before a
noun), or as a pronoun, with the meaning 'this,
that, the latter'. The declension is the same for
both uses.

	masc	*sing* fem	neut	*pl* all genders
nom	dieser	diese	dieses	diese
acc	diesen	diese	dieses	diese
gen	dieses(+s)	dieser	dieses(+s)	dieser
dat	diesem	dieser	diesem	diesen(+n)

  article: **kennen Sie diesen Mann?**
    do you know this man?
  geben Sie mir bitte diese Platte da
    would you give me that record there?
  pronoun: **diesen meine ich** I mean this one
  When 'dieser, diese, dieses' is used as an article,
any adjective coming between it and the noun

· ·

has the weak ADJECTIVE endings:

> **diese verdammten Touristen**
> these wretched tourists

There is also an uninflected form, **dies**, which is often used instead of 'dieses', especially as a pronoun:

> **dies hier ist mein Auto**
> this is my car here

diminutives are formed in German by adding either **-chen** or **-lein** to a noun to give the meaning 'little …'. If the noun has an **-a-, -o-,** or **-u-** in its stem, this usually gets an umlaut, and a noun ending in **-e** usually drops this 'e' before a diminutive ending. Both '-chen' and '-lein' make the noun neuter, no matter what gender it normally is:

der Kuß	das Küßchen	*little kiss*
die Jacke	das Jäckchen	*little jacket*
das Haus	das Häuschen	*little house*
das Kind	das Kindlein	*little child*

dir dative of 'du'. See PERSONAL PRONOUNS.

direct object case See ACCUSATIVE.

distance is expressed in the accusative when there is no preposition:

> **nur einen Kilometer außerhalb der Stadt**
> only one kilometre outside of town

doch 1. after all, anyway.

> **und jetzt hat sie es doch nicht gemacht**
> and now she hasn't done it after all

2. 'Doch' is very often used as a one-word reply to a question, when the answer is 'yes' but the questioner expects it to be 'no':

> **du willst nicht, oder? – doch!**
> you don't want to, do you? – oh yes (I do)

3. 'Doch' is also used with no particular meaning except to add emphasis:

> **das stimmt doch nicht!**
> that's just not true!

der Film ist doch so alt!
   (but) that film's so old
komm doch!
   oh, come on

dort   there. 'Dort' is only used with verbs of position; **dorthin** is used with verbs expressing movement to a place, and **dorther** with verbs expressing movement from a place.

dran, drauf, draus   *etc* are slightly informal versions of 'daran', 'darauf', 'daraus' etc.

du   you. See PERSONAL PRONOUNS.

durch   takes the accusative. See PREPOSITIONS.

durch-   is both a SEPARABLE PREFIX and an INSEPARABLE PREFIX. If the main stress falls on 'durch-', then it is separable; if the main stress falls on the actual verb, then it is inseparable:
   durchschauen (*insep*): **ich habe ihn gleich durchschaut** I saw what he was up to right away
   durchschauen (*sep*): **ich habe seinen Aufsatz flüchtig durchgeschaut** I looked quickly through his essay

dürfen   is a MODAL VERB meaning 'be allowed to, may'. Its principle parts are:
   dürfen, darf, durfte, gedurft/dürfen
and it uses 'haben' as its auxiliary. The present tense is irregular:

ich	darf	*wir*	dürfen
du	darfst	*ihr*	dürft
er, sie,		*Sie*	dürfen
es	darf	*sie*	dürfen

ehe   before. 'Ehe' is a CONJUNCTION that affects the word order of the sentence.

ein   has two functions in German. It is the indefinite article, corresponding to 'a' in English, but it can also be used as a pronoun meaning 'a man/woman/thing' *etc*. It has slightly different forms for each function.

◆I *The indefinite article*

	masc	fem	neut
nom	ein	eine	ein
acc	einen	eine	ein
gen	eines(+s)	einer	eines(+s)
dat	einem	einer	einem

An adjective coming between 'ein' and the noun has the mixed ADJECTIVE endings.

The indefinite article is used in much the same way in German as it is in English, but there are a few cases where it is not used:

1. if the noun tells you someone's profession or nationality, and comes after 'sein', 'werden', or 'bleiben':

> **er ist Engländer**
> he's English

> **sie wollte Ärztin werden**
> she wanted to be a doctor

but: **sie hat einen Franzosen geheiratet**
> she married a Frenchman

2. in certain idioms:

> **ich habe Kopfschmerzen**
> I've got a headache

3. after 'als' in uses like:

> **als Kind** as a child

> **als Student** as a student

There are also some nouns where German uses the indefinite article and English doesn't:

> **ein Wetter ist das heute!**
> some weather today!

> **da war vielleicht eine Hitze!**
> the heat there was just incredible!

◆II *Pronoun*

	masc	fem	neut
nom	einer	eine	ein(e)s
acc	einen	eine	ein(e)s
gen	eines	einer	eines
dat	einem	einer	einem

The pronoun is very often used to translate 'one of ...'. In this usage it can be followed either by the genitive, or by 'von' plus the dative. In the neuter nominative and accusative, the short form **eins** is just as acceptable as the longer form, and in fact is more common except in the 'one of ...' construction:

> **der Wagen gehört einem unserer Nachbarn** (*or* **einem von unseren Nachbarn**)
>> the car belongs to one of our neighbours
> **einer von euch** (*masc*)**, eine von euch** (*fem*)
>> one of you
> **ein(e)s der Kinder, ein(e)s von den Kindern**
>> one of the children
> **eins wollte ich noch sagen**
>> there was one other thing I wanted to say

ein- a SEPARABLE PREFIX which has the meaning 'in'. It is not used much with verbs of movement; **herein** and **hinein-** are generally used instead to express movement into a place:

> **einfahren: 'wird eingefahren'**
>> 'running in'

einig- can be used either as an article (that is, instead of 'a' or 'the' before a noun), or as a pronoun. In both uses it has the strong ADJECTIVE endings. Any adjective following it also has the strong endings, except in the masculine and neuter dative, where it is more common for a following adjective to have -en as its ending instead of -em.

> *adj:* **nach einiger Zeit** after some time
> **einige Male** several times
> **vor einigen Tagen** a few days ago
> *pronoun:* **das wird wohl einiges kosten**
>> that'll cost a bob or two
> **einige habe ich schon fertig**
>> I've already finished some of them

....

eins 1. neuter nominative and accusative of the pronoun EIN.
2. the number 'one'. See NUMBERS.

ent- an INSEPARABLE PREFIX which very often has the meaning 'de-':
> **entziffern: endlich gelang es mir, seine Schrift zu entziffern** at last I managed to decipher his handwriting

entgegen takes the dative. It usually comes after the noun or pronoun, rather than before it. See PREPOSITIONS.

entlang takes either the accusative or the dative, depending on its meaning. See PREPOSITIONS.

entweder ... oder either ... or. The alternatives can be single words:
> **entweder morgen oder übermorgen**
> either tomorrow or the day after

or they can be whole clauses, separated by a comma. In this case the word order of the first clause is very flexible:
> **ich lese entweder** (*or* **entweder ich lese** *or* **entweder lese ich**) **ein Buch, oder ich sehe fern**
> I either read a book or I watch television

er he; it. See PERSONAL PRONOUNS.

er- an INSEPARABLE PREFIX:
> **erfinden: das hat sie wohl erfunden**
> she must have invented that

-erweise is often added to adverbs to show that they are being used to comment on the whole sentence rather than just the verb. It can often be translated by 'enough':
> **eigenartigerweise wußte sie das nicht**
> strangely (enough), she didn't know that

es it; he; she. See PERSONAL PRONOUNS.

etwas is always neuter and never changes its form no matter what case it is in. It can be used in three slightly different ways:

  1. when used on its own or followed by an adjective used as a noun, 'etwas' usually means 'something' and is often replaced by the short form **was** in spoken and informal German. The adjective is written with a capital letter (with the exception of **etwas anderes**), and has the strong neuter adjective endings:

> **ich habe dir etwas mitgebracht**
>> I've brought something for you

> **ich habe etwas Schönes für dich**
>> I've something nice for you

  2. 'etwas' can also be used on its own to mean 'some, a bit'. Here again it can be replaced by **was**:

> **kann ich auch etwas davon haben?**
>> can I have some as well?

> **das wird schon etwas helfen**
>> that will help a bit

  3. 'etwas' can also mean 'some, a bit' when it is followed by a noun, an adjective, or an adverb:

> **es braucht noch etwas Salz**
>> it needs a bit more salt

> **das kam mir etwas komisch vor**
>> it seemed a bit funny to me

euch accusative and dative of 'ihr'. See PERSONAL PRONOUNS.

euer 1. your. See POSSESSIVES.
  2. genitive of 'ihr'. See PERSONAL PRONOUNS.

exclamations German exclamations are very often sentences starting with an INTERROGATIVE WORD:

> **was du nicht sagst!**
>> you don't say!

> **was für eine herrliche Aussicht!**
>> what a lovely view!

> **wie schön ist das!** *or* **wie schön das ist!**
>> isn't that nice!

....

wie schön du das gemacht hast! *or* **wie
schön hast du das gemacht!**
how nicely you've done it!
welch ein Glück!
what luck!
so eine Unverschämtheit!
what a cheek!

falls in case, if. 'Falls' is a CONJUNCTION that
affects the word order of the sentence.

feminine forms are used much more in
German than in English. The most common way
of forming the feminine is by adding **-in** to the
masculine form. If the masculine noun has an **-a-**,
-o-, or **-u-** in it, this usually gets an umlaut; if it is
a weak noun ending in **-e**, this 'e' is dropped:

der Arzt	die Ärztin	*doctor*
der Schüler	die Schülerin	*pupil*
der Franzose	die Französin	*French person*

Adjectives used as nouns simply have the
feminine endings when they refer to women:
ein Deutscher eine Deutsche *a German*

fern- a SEPARABLE PREFIX which often has the
meaning 'at a distance':
fernliegen: das lag mir fern
that was the last thing I had in mind

fest- a SEPARABLE PREFIX which often has the
meaning 'firmly, tightly':
festhalten: sie hielt an ihrem Glauben fest
she held fast to her faith

fort- a SEPARABLE PREFIX used with verbs of
movement with the meaning 'away', and with
other verbs with the meaning 'going on doing
something':
**fortlaufen: seine Freundin ist ihm
fortgelaufen** his girlfriend has left him
**fortsetzen: das wird nächste Woche
fortgesetzt** it will be continued next week

full stops   have two uses in German that differ from English usage.
   1. they are used to indicate thousands, millions etc:
   1.500.000 1,500,000
   2. they are used for ordinal numbers:
   1., 2., 3., 10. etc 1st, 2nd, 3rd, 10th etc
Otherwise uses are as in English.

für   takes the accusative. See PREPOSITIONS.

fürs   is a one-word contraction of 'für das'. It is used more in speech than in writing, and is never used when 'das' means 'that particular ...'. See AM for example.

future perfect tense   This corresponds in English to either 'I will (or shall) have met etc', or 'I will (or shall) have been dancing etc':
   **bis dahin wird er sie schon kennen-
      gelernt haben** by then he'll already have
      met her
   **ich werde den ganzen Abend getanzt
      haben** I'll have been dancing all evening
See the entry VERBS.

future tense   This corresponds in English to either 'I will (or shall) wait', or 'I am going to wait':
   wird sie auf dich warten?
      will she wait for you?
   ich werde nur ein paar Minuten warten
      I'll only wait (or I'm only going to wait) a
      few minutes
German quite often uses the present tense where English would use the future tense, especially in conversation:
   ich komme dich heute abend besuchen
      I'll come and see you this evening
See the entry VERBS.

ganz   can be used either as an adjective or an adverb. When it is an adjective it takes the ordinary weak, strong, or mixed ADJECTIVE

....

endings. Before the names of towns and countries, however, it has no ending at all:

ganz richtig
quite right
die ganze Stadt
the whole town
ganz München/Deutschland
the whole of Munich/Germany

ge- is used to form the past participle of practically all verbs except those which end in **-ieren**, or those which end in **-eien** and have a stem of more than one syllable, or those which start with an INSEPARABLE PREFIX. See VERBS.

gegen takes the accusative. See PREPOSITIONS.

gegenüber takes the dative. It usually comes before nouns, but after pronouns:

gegenüber der Kirche or **der Kirche gegenüber** opposite the church
mir gegenüber opposite me
See PREPOSITIONS.
An adverbial use is also possible:
gegenüber von der Kirche
opposite the church

gemäß takes the dative. It usually comes after the noun or pronoun, rather than before it. See PREPOSITIONS.

gender There are three genders in German – masculine, feminine, and neuter. These are grammatical genders, and they do not necessarily correspond to real life genders – for example, 'das Mädchen' (*girl*) is grammatically neuter. Every noun has a gender, and while it is not always possible to tell the gender of a noun from its meaning or form, there are some helpful rules and guidelines:
    1. Masculine:
    —days of the week;

—months of the year;
—the four seasons;
—points of the compass;
—the following endings:

-and	-eur	-ius
-ant	-graph	-ling
-er	-ich	-nom
-är	-ig	-oge
-ent *[1]	-ismus	-or
-er *[2]	-ist	-s *[3]

*[1] but not '-ment', which is neuter.
*[2] referring to people only, and excluding 'die
Mutter' and 'die Tochter'.
*[3] after a consonant, eg 'der Schnaps', but not
after a vowel.

2. Feminine:
—most trees;
—most flowers;
—most fruit (except 'der Apfel');
—most nouns ending in **-e**, except those which
refer to men and male animals, and those
which begin **Ge-**;
—the following endings:

-ade	-ette	-isse
-age	-euse	-ive
-anz	-heit	-keit
-atte	-ie	-schaft
-ei	-ik	-tät
-elle	-in *[2]	-ung
-enz	-ine	-ur
-esse*[1]	-ion	-üre

*[1] but 'das Interesse'.
*[2] but not chemicals.

3. Neuter:
—towns, cities and continents;
—infinitives used as nouns;
—collective nouns beginning with **Ge-**;
—nouns beginning with **Ge-** which are derived
from verbs (eg **Gerede** from 'reden', **Getue**
from 'tun');

···

—the following endings:

-at	-lein	-tel
-chen	-ment	-tum
-ett	-sel	-um

Articles such as 'der, die, das', 'ein', 'dieser' etc
always reflect the gender of the noun following
them, as do adjectives used in front of a noun.

Many pronouns also show gender, especially
the third person singular PERSONAL PRONOUNS,
and this gender is always the same as the noun
that is replaced by the pronoun:

> **der Schlüssel ... wo ist *er*?**
>> the key ... where is it?

> **welche Hose? ... *diese* hier**
>> which pair of trousers? ... this one here

genitive   The genitive is used:

1. as a way of showing possession, corresponding
to 'of' or '-'s':

> **das Auto *meiner Schwester***
>> my sister's car

> **die Einführung *neuer Methoden***
>> the introduction of new methods

> **zur Zeit *Goethes***
>> in the age of Goethe

The genitive is also expressed by the use of 'von'
with the dative:

> **die Einführung von neuen Methoden**
>> the introduction of new methods

> **die Welt von morgen**
>> the world of tomorrow

2. to express indefinite time:

> **eines Tages/Nachmittags**
>> one day/afternoon

3. after certain PREPOSITIONS.

4. instead of the accusative case with certain
verbs:

bedürfen	*require*
sich enthalten	*abstain from*
sich erinnern	*remember*
sich schämen	*be ashamed of*

5. with certain adjectives:

bewußt	*aware of*
fähig	*capable of*
müde *	*tired of*
schuldig	*guilty of*
sicher	*sure of*
überdrüssig	*weary of*
voll *	*full of*
wert *	*worth*
würdig	*worthy of*

* See also ACCUSATIVE (5).

6. In certain idioms, for example:

ich bin der Meinung, daß ...
I am of the opinion that ...

meines Erachtens
in my opinion

The only ordinary nouns to show a genitive ending are masculine and neuter. Those nouns which end in **-s, -ß, -z, -sch** and **-st** add '-es'; those which end in **-nis** add '-ses'; those which end in **-en, -em, -el, -er** or **-ling** add '-s'; and the others, apart from weak NOUNS, can add either '-s' or '-es'.

The names of people and places all show a genitive ending when they are used without an article, no matter what their gender. Usually this ending is '-s':

der Geburtsort Goethes
Goethe's birthplace

Marias Kleid
Maria's dress

die Bevölkerung Australiens
the population of Australia

An apostrophe is used instead of '-s' for names which end in **-s, -ß** or **-tz**, but this tends to be rather formal. It is more usual to turn the phrase round and use 'von' or an article.

Perikles' Tod
the death of Pericles

die Musik von Sibelius
the music of Sibelius

....

7. After personal names with an article the genitive does not add '-s':

die Musik eines Beethoven
the music of a Beethoven

geographical names   See COUNTRIES and PLACE NAMES.

gerunds   See -ING FORMS.

gleich   takes the dative. See PREPOSITIONS.

haben   is an ordinary transitive verb as well as being one of the AUXILIARY VERBS. Its principle parts are:

haben, hat, hatte, gehabt
and it uses 'haben' as its auxiliary.

	present tense	*present subjunctive*
ich	habe	habe
du	hast	habest
er, sie, es	hat	habe
wir	haben	haben
ihr	habt	habet
Sie	haben	haben
sie	haben	haben
	imperfect tense	*imperfect subjunctive*
ich	hatte	hätte
du	hattest	hättest
er, sie, es	hatte	hätte
wir	hatten	hätten
ihr	hattet	hättet
Sie	hatten	hätten
sie	hatten	hätten

perfect tense
   ich habe gehabt
         etc
imperative
   (*'du' form*)   habe *or* hab
   (*'ihr' form*)   habt
   (*'Sie' form*)   haben Sie

her is an adverb which is used mainly in phrases without a verb; if there is a verb, the prefix **her-** is generally used instead. It has no exact translation in English, but its general meaning is 'moving here, towards the speaker'. It is very often used with a preposition:

vom Süden her
from the south
von weit her
from far away
um mich her
all around me
her mit dem Geld!
give me the money!

her- 1. a SEPARABLE PREFIX used with verbs of movement with the general meaning 'to where the speaker is':

herfinden: hast du gleich hergefunden?
did you find your way straight here?

2. a prefix used with adverbs and prepositions of place, which adds the sense 'to where the speaker is':

herauf (*adverb*): **vom Tal herauf**
up from the valley (*when the speaker is on the mountain*)
(*preposition*): **die Treppe herauf**
up the stairs (*when the speaker is upstairs*)

3. 'her-' also combines with SEPARABLE PREFIXES, again with the same general meaning. When this happens, 'her-' and the prefix can be separated from the verb, but never from each other:

herüberkommen: wie sind sie über den Fluß herübergekommen?
how did they get across the river (*to our side*)?

hin is an adverb which is used mainly in phrases without a verb; if there is a verb, the prefix **hin-** is generally used instead. It has no exact translation in English, but its general

meaning is 'moving away from the speaker'. It is
very often used in combination with a preposition:

nach Süden hin
to the south
zur anderen Seite hin
to the other side

hin-   1. a SEPARABLE PREFIX used with verbs of
movement with the meaning 'away from where
the speaker is':

hingehen: ich ging sofort hin
I went there straight away

2. a prefix used with adverbs and prepositions of
place, which adds the sense 'away from where the
speaker is':

hinauf (*adverb*): **zum Berg hinauf**
up to the mountain (*when the speaker is in
the valley*)
(*preposition*): **die Treppe hinauf**
up the stairs (*when the speaker is
downstairs*)

3. 'hin-' also combines with SEPARABLE PREFIXES,
again with the same general meaning. When this
happens, 'hin-' and the prefix can be separated
from the verb, but never from each other:

**hinausschauen: ich schaute zum Fenster
hinaus** I looked out of the window

hinten   is an adverb meaning 'behind, at the
back'. It should not be confused with **hinter**.

hinter   is a PREPOSITION which takes either the
accusative or the dative, depending on whether it
is expressing movement or not. It should not be
confused with **hinten**, which is an adverb.

hinterm, hintern, hinters   These are
one-word contractions of 'hinter dem', 'hinter
den', and 'hinter das'. They are used more in
speech than in writing, and are never used when
'dem', 'den', or 'das' means 'that particular ...'. See
AM for example.

hyphenation There are very strict rules in German about where a word can be split.

1. Words of one syllable are never split.

2. Compounds are best split between the two elements (though the other rules given here still apply). If there are linking letters (-e-, -en-, -er-, -es-, -n-, or -s-) between the two elements, these go with the first element:

die Fremd-sprache	*foreign language*
die Studenten-kneipe	*student pub*
das Kinder-spiel	*children's game*

3. For words which are not compounds, the general rule is that if there are two consonants then the split comes between them, if there are three consonants then the split comes before the last one, and if there is only one consonant then the split is made before it. There are some consonant combinations which count as a single consonant for the purposes of hyphenation; these are **-ch-**, **-sch-**, **-st-**, **-ph-**, and **-ß-**, and **-ss-** when it stands for **-ß-**. These latter consonant groups must never be split:

die Sil-be	*syllable*
war-ten	*wait*
müs-sen	*must*
die Män-ner	*men*
kämp-fen	*fight*
na-hen	*approach*
die Bü-cher	*books*
der Mei-ster	*master*
der Geburts-tag	*birthday*

It is possible to split **-ck-**, but if it is split then the **-c-** is replaced by **-k-**:

der Zuk-ker	*sugar*
der Bäk-ker	*baker*

4. If there are no consonants between syllables it is possible to split between two vowels, but only if they are pronounced quite distinctly from each other and are not diphthongs:

die Trau-ung	*wedding*

....

5. The fact that a particular syllable might be an inflectional ending is irrelevant in determining where a word can be split. But if a word begins with a prefix then the rules above do not apply and it is acceptable to split immediately after the prefix:

aus-atmen	*breathe out*
ver-ewigen	*immortalize*
ge-sprungen	*jumped*
Ge-schmack	*taste*

ich I. See PERSONAL PRONOUNS.
ich bin's it's me

ihm dative of 'er' and 'es'. See PERSONAL PRONOUNS.

ihn accusative of 'er'. See PERSONAL PRONOUNS.

Ihnen dative of 'Sie'. See PERSONAL PRONOUNS.

ihnen dative of 'sie'. See PERSONAL PRONOUNS.

ihr 1. you. See PERSONAL PRONOUNS.
2. her, its; their. See POSSESSIVES.

Ihr 1. you, only written with a capital letter in correspondence. See PERSONAL PRONOUNS.
2. your (polite). See POSSESSIVES.

im is a one-word contraction of 'in dem'. It usually replaces the full form except where 'dem' means 'that particular ...'. See AM for example. It is always used instead of the full form in certain fixed phrases or when it is followed by an infinitive used as a noun:
ganz im Gegenteil
just the opposite
im Radio
on the radio
im Mai
in May
das habe ich im Sitzen gemacht
I did it sitting down

imperatives　There are three forms of the second person imperative in German, corresponding to 'du', 'ihr', and 'Sie', as well as various possibilities for expressing the first person plural imperative.

1. The 'du' form

For the vast majority of weak verbs, and for strong verbs whose stem vowel does not change to -i- or -ie-, the imperative is either the verb stem alone or the verb stem with an -e on the end. In most cases it is slightly more formal to add -e, otherwise there is no difference between the two forms:

komm her!
　　come here!
trink mal schnell aus!
　　drink up quickly!

Verbs which end in -eln or -ern always add -e to the end of the stem, but the -e- which is part of the stem itself may be dropped:

läch(e)le mal schön!
　　smile nicely!

Verbs which end in -ten, -den, -chnen, -cknen, -dnen, -fnen, -gnen, or -tmen always add -e to the stem:

rechne es mal zusammen!
　　add it up!
atme langsam!
　　breathe slowly!

Strong verbs whose stem vowel changes to -i- or -ie- in the second and third person singular, form the imperative by using the second person singular, present tense, without the -st ending. No -e is added:

nimm dir!
　　help yourself
lies doch nicht so schnell!
　　don't read so quickly!

The imperative of 'sein' is irregular:
sei still! be quiet!

2. The 'ihr' form

For all verbs, whether weak or strong, the second person plural imperative is exactly the same as the second person plural, present tense, except that no pronoun is used:

> **sagt mir Bescheid, wann ihr kommen wollt!** let me know when you want to come

3. The 'Sie' form

The polite second person imperative is the same as the polite second person, present tense, for all verbs except 'sein', except that the order of the pronoun and the verb is inverted:

> **rufen Sie mich mal an!**
> give me a ring some time

The imperative of 'sein' is irregular:

> **seien Sie nicht böse!**
> don't be angry

4. The imperative can also be formed by using the infinitive:

> **nicht berühren!** do not touch
> **nicht weinen!** don't cry

The past participle can also be used as an imperative:

> **aufgestanden!** get up!

This latter construction can easily sound very curt.

5. The 'wir' form

The most straightforward form of the first person plural imperative is simply the use of the first person plural, present tense, with the pronoun and the verb in reverse order:

> **gehen wir!**
> let's go

But there are other ways of expressing the same idea:

> **komm/kommt/kommen Sie, wir wollen gehen!** come on, let's go

or rather more formally:

> **laß/laßt/lassen Sie uns gehen!**
> let's go

laßt uns beten! let us pray
Whether you use the 'du', 'ihr', or 'Sie' form
depends on the way you usually address the other
person or people who make up the 'we'.

imperfect tense 1. This corresponds in
English to either 'I wrote', or 'I used to write', or 'I
was writing':

er schrieb einen Brief
he wrote a letter
er schrieb mir jeden Tag he wrote to me (*or*
he used to write to me) every day
**er schrieb gerade einen Brief, als ich
hereinkam**
he was writing a letter when I came in

The imperfect is the tense that is generally used
in writing in German, not the perfect tense. See
the entry VERBS.
2. Note the following use of the imperfect tense
in German:

**er ging schon seit Jahren in dieselbe
Kneipe**
he had been going to the same pub for years
wie lange warst du schon da?
how long had you been there?

impersonal verbs in German fall into
several groups.
1. Verbs connected with the weather are always
impersonal, as they are in English:

es regnet/hagelt/schneit
it's raining/hailing/snowing
es hat geblitzt
there was lightning
es dämmert
dawn is breaking (*or* dusk is falling)
2. Verbs connected with sound are often used
impersonally if it is not known exactly who or
what is making the noise:

es klingelt an der Tür
that's the doorbell

3. Some verbs, especially those connected with mental impressions or physical sensations, have an impersonal subject but use a personal pronoun as either the direct object or the indirect object:

es gefällt mir nicht
I don't like it

es freut mich, daß Sie gekommen sind
I'm glad you've come

wie geht es Ihnen?
how are you?

In some cases the 'es' can be omitted:

es fällt mir ein, daß... *or* **mir fällt ein, daß ...**
it occurs to me that ...

mich friert
I'm cold

4. Many verbs of action can also be used impersonally. If the most important thing is simply that the action takes place, rather than that a particular person carries it out, an impersonal form of the passive can be used:

es wurde viel getanzt
there was a lot of dancing

es wird dort viel getrunken
people drink a lot there

5. There are also many verbs which are used impersonally in set phrases:

das macht nichts
it doesn't matter

es geschieht ihm recht
it serves him right

mir ist warm/kalt
I'm hot/cold

in takes either the accusative or the dative, depending on whether it is expressing movement or not. See PREPOSITIONS.

-in See FEMININE FORMS.

indem while, as. 'Indem' is a CONJUNCTION that affects the word order of the sentence.

indirect object case   See DATIVE.

indirect speech   is usually in the
SUBJUNCTIVE, except when it is introduced by 'daß'
and there is no doubt about the truth of the
statement being reported:

man hat mir gesagt, daß sie krank ist
someone told me that she is ill (*and that is
definitely true*)

man hat mir gesagt, daß sie krank sei
someone told me that she is (*or* was) ill (*but
I don't know whether that's true*)

The verb in direct speech is 'translated' into
indirect speech according to the following pattern
of tenses:

Direct Speech	Indirect Speech
present	present subjunctive *or* imperfect subjunctive
imperfect	perfect subjunctive *or* pluperfect subjunctive
perfect	perfect subjunctive *or* pluperfect subjunctive
pluperfect	perfect subjunctive *or* pluperfect subjunctive
future	future subjunctive *or* conditional
conditional	future subjunctive *or* conditional

When choosing which tense to use, the most
important factor is that it should be clear that the
verb is subjunctive. As the present and perfect
subjunctives of most verbs only differ from the
ordinary present and perfect tenses in the third
person singular, one would usually select the
imperfect subjunctive or the pluperfect
subjunctive instead, for all the persons other than
the third person singular. The main exception is
'sein', which has distinct subjunctive forms:

sie sagte, er hätte (*or* habe) keine Zeit
she said that he didn't have time

sie sagte, du hättest keine Zeit
she said that you didn't have time
man hat mir gesagt, du seist (*or* **wär(e)st**)
böse mit mir someone told me you were
angry with me

infinitives The infinitive is the form of the
verb which is given in dictionaries. It always ends
in **-en** or **-n**, and its general meaning is 'to ...'.

◆I *Use with* **zu**.

In the same way that English infinitives often
have 'to' in front of them, German infinitives often
have 'zu':

wir haben beschlossen, morgen zu
kommen we decided to come tomorrow
ihr Ziel war, Ärztin zu werden
her ambition was to be a doctor

If the infinitive starts with a SEPARABLE PREFIX,
the 'zu' is put between the prefix and the rest of
the infinitive:

Birgit hat mich gebeten, ihre Eltern
anzurufen
Birgit asked me to phone her parents

'Zu' is not used in the following situations:

1. when the infinitive is used to form the future
and conditional tenses:

ich werde es ihm sagen
I'll tell him

2. with a MODAL VERB:

ich kann leider nicht mitkommen
I'm afraid I can't come with you
das hätte sie nicht machen dürfen
she shouldn't have done that

3. with 'bleiben', 'finden', 'fühlen', 'gehen', 'hören',
'lassen', 'machen', and 'sehen':

sie hat mich nicht schwimmen gehen
lassen
she wouldn't let me go swimming
ich gehe jetzt schlafen
I'm going to go to bed now

hast du sie tanzen sehen?
have you seen her dance?
4. with 'heißen', 'helfen', 'lehren', or 'lernen', if the infinitive stands on its own:
er half mir aufräumen
he helped me (to) clear up
But if the infinitive is expanded in any way then 'zu' is used:
er half mir, alles wegzuräumen
he helped me (to) clear everything away
5. when the infinitive is the subject of the sentence:
arbeiten kann ja Spaß machen
work can be fun
'Zu' is always used when the infinitive follows 'ohne', 'statt', or 'anstatt':
er grüßte uns, ohne uns anzusehen
he said hallo without looking at us
anstatt den LKW zu überholen, fuhr er plötzlich langsamer instead of overtaking the lorry he suddenly slowed down

◆II *Use with* **um ... zu**
When the English infinitive is used to mean 'in order to' or 'so that', it is usually translated into German by 'um ... zu' and the infinitive:
sie schickte mich zum Postamt, um Briefmarken zu kaufen she sent me to the post office to buy stamps
Sie werden nicht bezahlt, um Zeitung zu lesen, sondern um zu arbeiten
you are paid to work, not to read the papers
The construction with 'um ... zu' is also used to translate the English 'too ... to':
es war zu kalt, um eine Grillparty zu geben it was too cold to have a barbecue

◆III *Use as a noun*
All German infinitives can be written with a capital letter and used as a neuter noun, very often corresponding to the English **-ing** form:

das Schwimmen swimming
das Atmen der Kinder the children's
      breathing
This is done especially often when there is a
preposition in front of the infinitive:
ich habe keine Zeit zum Fernsehen
      I've no time to watch (*or* for watching)
      television
Ulli war gerade beim Bügeln
      Ulli was just (doing the) ironing
ihre Freude am Tanzen
      the pleasure she gets from dancing
eine Tasche zum Büchertragen
      a bag for carrying books

-ing forms   are translated into German in a
number of ways:
   1. When an English '-ing' form is used as an
adjective, the German equivalent is very often the
PRESENT PARTICIPLE, also used as an adjective:
eine dauernde Freundschaft
      a lasting friendship
   2. When the English '-ing' form is used as a noun
the German equivalent is often an infinitive used
as a noun; see INFINITIVES III.
   3. After 'bleiben', 'finden', 'fühlen', 'gehen',
'hören', 'lassen', and 'sehen', an '-ing' form is often
translated by the infinitive without 'zu',
especially if it stands on its own rather than
introducing another section of the sentence:
sie blieb dort stehen
      she stayed standing there
würdest du lieber tanzen gehen?
      would you rather go dancing?
ich habe dich kommen hören/sehen
      I heard/saw you coming
After 'fühlen', 'hören', 'sehen', and other verbs
which describe physical or mental sensations, an
'-ing' form which introduces another section of the
sentence is often translated by a new clause
beginning with 'wie':

**ich habe gehört, wie du die Treppe
    heraufgekommen bist** I heard you
    coming up the stairs
4. Other ways of translating '-ing' forms are:
**sie ging an mir vorbei, ohne mich zu
    sehen** she went past without seeing me
ich hatte vor, nach Frankreich zu fahren
    I intended going to France
**nachdem sie sich geduscht hatte, zog sie
    sich an**
    after having a shower she got dressed
**weil ich so faul bin, schreibe ich nur
    selten Briefe** being rather lazy, I don't
    often write letters
sie kam auf mich zugelaufen
    she came running up to me
spielst du gern Fußball?
    do you like playing football?
morgens trinke ich lieber Kaffee
    I prefer drinking coffee in the morning

innerhalb   takes the genitive. See
PREPOSITIONS.

ins   is a one-word contraction of 'in das'. It
usually replaces the full form except where 'das'
means 'that particular ...'. See AM for example.

inseparable prefixes   are prefixes which
are put at the beginning of the verb and which are
then never separated from the rest of the verb.
The only way in which a verb starting with an
inseparable prefix differs from an ordinary verb is
that there is no **ge-** in the past participle, either at
the beginning or in the middle:
beschließen – beschlossen decide – decided
The main inseparable prefixes are:
be-   dis-   ent-   er-
miß-   ver-   zer-
In addition, DURCH-, ÜBER-, UM-, UNTER- and
WIEDER- are sometimes, but not always,
inseparable.

interrogative sentences   See QUESTIONS.

interrogative words   cause the subject of
the sentence and the verb to be inverted:

> **wann kommt er?**
>> when is he coming?
>
> **um wieviel Uhr kommt er?**
>> what time is he coming (at)?

Interrogative words can also be used in
sentences which contain a question in INDIRECT
SPEECH. In this case they introduce a SUBORDINATE
CLAUSE which should be separated off by commas
and have its verb at the end:

> **ich weiß nicht, wann er kommt**
>> I don't know when he's coming
>
> **ich verstehe nicht, warum sie das macht**
>> I don't understand why she does that

There are three classes of interrogative words:

1. Adverbs

wann	*when*
warum	*why*
weshalb	*why*
weswegen	*why*
wie	*how*
wie lange	*how long*
wie oft	*how often*
wieso	*why, how come*
wo	*where*
wo(r)-+prep	*where ..., what ...*
eg woher	*where from*
wohin	*where (to)*
woraus	*what ... of*
etc	

2. Pronouns

was	*what*
was für einer/ eine/eins	*what sort of person/thing*
welcher, welche, welches	*who, which*
wer	*who*

Interrogative pronouns have to be declined; you will find their declensions under their own entries, but there are two points to note. Firstly, the plural form of 'was für einer' is 'was für welche'; and secondly, there is no dative of 'was'. Instead, a special form 'wo-' (or 'wor-' before vowels) is used, which combines with a preposition. This form can also be used with prepositions which take the accusative. Like all pronouns, interrogative pronouns have the same NUMBER and GENDER as the noun they refer back to, but their case depends on the function they have in their own sentence or clause:

> **du hast jetzt ein Auto? was für eins?**
>> you've got a car now? what sort?
>
> **wem schreibst du?**
>> who are you writing to?
>
> **wozu dient das?**
>> what is that used for?

3. Adjectives

> was für ein/eine/ein   *what sort of*
> welcher, welche, welches   *which, what*

These also have to be declined, and you will find their declensions in their own entries. Note, however, that as an adjective the plural form of 'was für ein' is simply 'was für':

> **welches Kleid soll ich anziehen?**
>> which dress shall I wear?
>
> **was für Leute sind das?**
>> what sort of people are they?

inverted commas are used in the same way as in English, but are written and printed differently:

> **dann sagte sie: „warum nicht?"**
>> then she said, 'why not?'

irgend is an adverb meaning 'some'. It never changes its form, but it is usually written as one word with the pronoun or adverb after it except when this is 'jemand' or 'etwas':

irgend jemand hat das bestimmt gesehen
someone (or other) must have seen it
sie hat mir irgend etwas (*or* irgendwas)
erzählt she told me something or other
es muß doch hier irgendwo liegen
it must be here somewhere

irregular verbs This is a list of the
principle parts of all the common strong and
mixed verbs. Any verb which starts with a
SEPARABLE PREFIX followed by one of these verbs
will have the same principle parts. Any verb
which starts with an INSEPARABLE PREFIX followed
by one of these verbs will also have the same
principle parts preceded by the prefix, but without
the **ge-** in the past participle.

Verbs marked * always use 'sein' as their
auxiliary. Those marked (*) use 'sein' only when
they are intransitive; when they are transitive
they use 'haben'.

infinitive	3rd person sing present	3rd person sing imperf	past participle
backen	bäckt, backt	backte	gebacken
befehlen	befiehlt	befahl	befohlen
beginnen	beginnt	begann	begonnen
beißen	beißt	biß	gebissen
bersten*	birst	barst	geborsten
betrügen	betrügt	betrog	betrogen
bewegen (=*cause*)	bewegt	bewog	bewogen
biegen(*)	biegt	bog	gebogen
bieten	bietet	bot	geboten
binden	bindet	band	gebunden
bitten	bittet	bat	gebeten
blasen	bläst	blies	geblasen
bleiben*	bleibt	blieb	geblieben
braten	brät	briet	gebraten
brechen(*)	bricht	brach	gebrochen
brennen	brennt	brannte	gebrannt
bringen	bringt	brachte	gebracht
denken	denkt	dachte	gedacht
dringen(*)	dringt	drang	gedrungen
dürfen	darf	durfte	dürfen/gedurft

empfehlen	empfiehlt	empfahl	empfohlen
erlöschen*	erlischt	erlosch	erloschen
erschrecken*	erschrickt	erschrak	erschrocken
erwägen	erwägt	erwog	erwogen
essen	ißt	aß	gegessen
fahren(*)	fährt	fuhr	gefahren
fallen*	fällt	fiel	gefallen
fangen	fängt	fing	gefangen
fechten	ficht	focht	gefochten
finden	findet	fand	gefunden
flechten	flicht	flocht	geflochten
fliegen(*)	fliegt	flog	geflogen
fliehen(*)	flieht	floh	geflohen
fließen*	fließt	floß	geflossen
fressen	frißt	fraß	gefressen
frieren(*)	friert	fror	gefroren
gebären	gebiert	gebar	geboren
geben	gibt	gab	gegeben
gedeihen*	gedeiht	gedieh	gediehen
gehen*	geht	ging	gegangen
gelingen*	gelingt	gelang	gelungen
gelten	gilt	galt	gegolten
genesen*	genest	genas	genesen
genießen	genießt	genoß	genossen
geschehen*	geschieht	geschah	geschehen
gewinnen	gewinnt	gewann	gewonnen
gießen	gießt	goß	gegossen
gleichen	gleicht	glich	geglichen
gleiten*	gleitet	glitt	geglitten
graben	gräbt	grub	gegraben
greifen	greift	griff	gegriffen
haben	hat	hatte	gehabt
halten	hält	hielt	gehalten
hängen	hängt	hing	gehangen
hauen	haut	haute	gehauen
heben	hebt	hob	gehoben
hießen	heißt	hieß	geheißen
helfen	hilft	half	geholfen
kennen	kennt	kannte	gekannt
klingen	klingt	klang	geklungen
kneifen	kneift	kniff	gekniffen
kommen*	kommt	kam	gekommen
können	kann	konnte	können/gekonnt
kriechen*	kriecht	kroch	gekrochen
laden	lädt	lud	geladen
lassen	läßt	ließ	lassen/gelassen

laufen*	läuft	lief	gelaufen
leiden	leidet	litt	gelitten
leihen	leiht	lieh	geliehen
lesen	liest	las	gelesen
liegen	liegt	lag	gelegen
lügen	lügt	log	gelogen
mahlen	mahlt	mahlte	gemahlen
meiden	meidet	mied	gemieden
messen	mißt	maß	gemessen
mißlingen	mißlingt	mißlang	mißlungen
mögen	mag	mochte	mögen/gemocht
müssen	mußt	mußte	müssen/gemußt
nehmen	nimmt	nahm	genommen
nennen	nennt	nannte	genannt
pfeifen	pfeift	pfiff	gepfiffen
preisen	preist	pries	gepriesen
quellen*	quillt	quoll	gequollen
raten	rät	riet	geraten
reiben	reibt	rieb	gerieben
reißen(*)	reißt	riß	gerissen
reiten(*)	reitet	ritt	geritten
rennen*	rennt	rannte	gerannt
riechen	riecht	roch	gerochen
ringen	ringt	rang	gerungen
rinnen*	rinnt	rann	geronnen
rufen	ruft	rief	gerufen
salzen	salzt	salzte	gesalzen
saufen	säuft	soff	gesoffen
saugen	saugt	sog	gesogen
schaffen	schafft	schuf	geschaffen
scheiden(*)	scheidet	schied	geschieden
scheinen	scheint	schien	geschienen
schelten	schilt	schalt	gescholten
schieben	schiebt	schob	geschoben
schießen(*)	schießt	schoß	geschossen
schlafen	schläft	schlief	geschlafen
schlagen	schlägt	schlug	geschlagen
schleichen*	schleicht	schlich	geschlichen
schleifen	schleift	schliff	geschliffen
schließen	schließt	schloß	geschlossen
schlingen	schlingt	schlang	geschlungen
schmeißen	schmeißt	schmiß	geschmissen
schmelzen(*)	schmilzt	schmolz	geschmolzen
schneiden	schneidet	schnitt	geschnitten
schreiben	schreibt	schrieb	geschrieben
schreien	schreit	schrie	geschrie(e)n

....

schreiten*	schreitet	schritt	geschritten
schweigen	schweigt	schwieg	geschwiegen
schwellen*	schwillt	schwoll	geschwollen
schwimmen(*)	schwimmt	schwamm	geschwommen
schwingen	schwingt	schwang	geschwungen
schwören	schwört	schwor	geschworen
sehen	sieht	sah	gesehen
sein*	ist	war	gewesen
senden	sendet	sendete	gesendet
		sandte	gesandt
singen	singt	sang	gesungen
sinken*	sinkt	sank	gesunken
sinnen	sinnt	sann	gesonnen
sitzen	sitzt	saß	gesessen
sollen	soll	sollte	sollen/gesollt
speien	speit	spie	gespie(e)n
spinnen	spinnt	spann	gesponnen
sprechen	spricht	sprach	gesprochen
sprießen*	sprießt	sproß	gesprossen
springen*	springt	sprang	gesprungen
stechen	sticht	stach	gestochen
stehen	steht	stand	gestanden
stehlen	stiehlt	stahl	gestohlen
steigen*	steigt	stieg	gestiegen
sterben*	stirbt	starb	gestorben
stinken	stinkt	stank	gestunken
stoßen(*)	stößt	stieß	gestoßen
streichen(*)	streicht	strich	gestrichen
streiten	streitet	stritt	gestritten
tragen	trägt	trug	getragen
treffen	trifft	traf	getroffen
treiben(*)	treibt	trieb	getrieben
treten(*)	tritt	trat	getreten
trinken	trinkt	trank	getrunken
tun	tut	tat	getan
verbergen	verbirgt	verbarg	verborgen
verderben(*)	verdirbt	verdarb	verdorben
vergessen	vergißt	vergaß	vergessen
verlieren	verliert	verlor	verloren
vermeiden	vermeidet	vermied	vermieden
verschwinden*	verschwindet	verschwand	verschwunden
verzeihen	verzeiht	verzieh	verziehen
wachsen*	wächst	wuchs	gewachsen
waschen	wäscht	wusch	gewaschen
weben	webt	webte,	gewebt,
		wob	gewoben

weichen*	weicht	wich	gewichen
weisen	weist	wies	gewiesen
wenden	wendet	wendete, wandte	gewendet, gewandt
werben	wirbt	warb	geworben
werden*	wird	wurde	geworden
werfen	wirft	warf	geworfen
wiegen	wiegt	wog	gewogen
winden	windet	wand	gewunden
wissen	weiß	wußte	gewußt
wollen	will	wollte	wollen/gewollt
ziehen(*)	zieht	zog	gezogen
zwingen	zwingt	zwang	gezwungen

it is not always 'es' in German; it may also be 'er' or 'sie'. Gender in German is grammatical not factual, and the pronoun chosen to translate 'it' should be the same grammatical gender as the noun it replaces:

> **mein Aufsatz ... ich habe *ihn* noch nicht geschrieben** my essay ... I haven't written it yet
>
> **deine Uhr ... ich habe *sie* nicht** your watch ... I haven't got it

ja is often used as a 'filler word':

> **das war ja dumm**
>   that was (pretty) stupid
> **das ist es ja!**
>   that's just it!
> **das ist ja viel besser**
>   that's much better

je..., desto ... (*or* **um so**) If there are verbs involved, the verb in the first part of the sentence is sent to the end of the clause, and the verb in the second is inverted with the subject. There must be a comma between the two parts of the sentence:

> **je eher, desto** (*or* **um so**) **besser**
>   the sooner the better
> **je älter ich werde, desto** (*or* **um so**) **unsicherer werde ich**
>   the older I get, the less confident I become

jeder, jede, jedes can be used either as an article (that is, instead of 'a' or 'the' before a noun), or as a pronoun, with the meaning 'every, each; everybody, each one'. The declension is the same for both uses:

	masc	fem	neut
nom	jeder	jede	jedes
acc	jeden	jede	jedes
gen	jedes(+s)	jeder	jedes(+s)
dat	jedem	jeder	jedem

article: **jedes Kind**
> every *or* each child

so was passiert doch nicht jeden Tag
> things like that don't happen every day

es könnte jeden Augenblick passieren
> it could happen (at) any moment

pronoun: **jeder weiß das**
> everybody knows that

er hat jedem von uns was gegeben
> he gave something to each of us

jedem das Seine
> each to his own

When 'jeder, jede, jedes' is used as an article, any adjective coming between it and the noun has the weak ADJECTIVE endings:

jeder zweite Tag
> every second day

jemand somebody. 'Jemand' usually declines:

nom	jemand
acc	jemand(en)
gen	jemand(e)s
dat	jemandem

In the accusative the ending is very often left off, especially in speech.

When 'jemand' is followed by 'ander(e)s', it does not have any ending, no matter what case it is:

das habe ich von jemand ander(e)m gehört I heard that from somebody else

....

'Jemand' can also be followed by an adjective used as a neuter noun. Again, it never changes its form:
der Brief war wohl von jemand Fremdem geschrieben the letter was probably written by somebody he/she didn't know

jener, jene, jenes   can be used either as an article (that is, instead of 'a' or 'the' before a noun), or as a pronoun, with the meaning 'that (one), the former'. The declension is the same for both uses:

	sing masc	*fem*	*neut*	*pl* all genders
nom	jener	jene	jenes	jene
acc	jenen	jene	jenes	jene
gen	jenes(+s)	jener	jenes(+s)	jener
dat	jenem	jener	jenem	jenen(+n)

'Jener, jene, jenes' is not used as much as 'that' in English; 'dieser, diese, dieses' is more commonly used instead. 'Jener, jene, jenes' is used mainly when there is an explicit contrast between 'this' and 'that', or to refer to some distant thing or time:
die Erinnerungen an jene finsteren Tage the memories of those dark days
When 'jener, jene, jenes' is used as an article, any adjective coming between it and the noun has the weak ADJECTIVE endings.

jenseits   takes the genitive. See PREPOSITIONS.

kein   has two functions in German. It is the negative of the indefinite article, corresponding to 'not a' in English, and it can also be used as a pronoun meaning 'nobody, nothing'. It has slightly different forms for each function.

◆I *The negative indefinite article*

	sing masc	*fem*	*neut*	*pl* all genders
nom	kein	keine	kein	keine
acc	keinen	keine	kein	keine
gen	keines(+s)	keiner	keines(+s)	keiner
dat	keinem	keiner	keinem	keinen(+n)

An adjective coming between 'kein' and the noun after it has the mixed ADJECTIVE endings:

ich habe kein einziges Mädchen gesehen
I didn't see a single girl

das wäre keine schlechte Idee
that wouldn't be a bad idea

das ist noch keine fünf Minuten her
it was less than five minutes ago

'Nicht ein' can be used for emphasis:

nicht eine Mark hatte er *or* **er hatte keine einzige Mark** he didn't have a single mark

◆ II *Pronoun*

	masc	sing fem	neut	pl all genders
nom	keiner	keine	kein(e)s	keine
acc	keinen	keine	kein(e)s	keine
gen	—	—	—	—
dat	keinem	keiner	keinem	keinen

Like all pronouns, 'keiner, keine, kein(e)s' always has the same gender and number as the noun it replaces, but its case depends on its own function in the sentence:

es war keiner da there was nobody there
(=not a single person)

es waren keine da
there was nobody there (=no people)

Kaffee? es ist keiner da
coffee? there isn't any

Bücher? es sind keine da
books? there aren't any

ich habe kein(e)s
I haven't got one

keiner von uns beiden
neither of us

können is a MODAL VERB meaning 'can, be able to'. Its principle parts are:

können, kann, konnte, gekonnt/können
and it uses 'haben' as its auxiliary. The present tense is irregular:

ich	kann	*wir*	können
du	kannst	*ihr*	könnt
er, sie,		*Sie*	können
es	kann	*sie*	können

languages   There are three forms that are
used in German to translate the name of a
language; in the case of 'German' itself, these are
das Deutsche (declined as an adjective), **(das)
Deutsch,** and **deutsch.** (The names of other
languages follow the same pattern.) These three
forms are not used interchangeably, but
correspond roughly to the following ideas in
English:

1. the German language in general=**das
Deutsche**
   ins Deutsche übersetzt
      translated into German
   aus dem Deutschen übersetzt
      translated from (the) German
   die Formen des Verbs im Deutschen
      the forms of the verb in German
2. a particular type of German, or a particular
person's ability to speak German=**(das) Deutsch**
   in modernem Deutsch
      in modern German
   sie spricht (ein) sehr gutes Deutsch
      her German is very good
   er spricht kein Deutsch
      he doesn't speak any German
3. German being spoken as the language of
communication=**deutsch**
   sie sprachen deutsch
      they were speaking German
   wir unterhielten uns auf deutsch
      we were talking (in) German
   wie heißt das auf deutsch?
      what's that in German?

lassen   In the sense of 'to let, to allow, to have
something done', 'lassen' behaves like a MODAL

VERB; in the sense of 'to leave', however, it is
simply an irregular verb. Its principle parts are:
 lassen, läßt, ließ, gelassen/lassen
and it uses 'haben' as its auxiliary. The present
tense is irregular:

ich	lasse	wir	lassen
du	läßt	ihr	laßt
er, sie,		Sie	lassen
es	läßt	sie	lassen

imperative
 ('*du*' *form*) laß
 ('*ihr*' *form*) laßt
 ('*Sie*' *form*) lassen Sie

   Like the modal verbs, 'lassen' has two past
participles. **Gelassen** is only used when there is
no infinitive of another verb in the sentence,
which means that it is used mainly in the sense of
'left'. If there is an infinitive of another verb, as is
usually the case in the sense of 'let', 'allowed', 'had
done', **lassen** is used:
   ich habe es zu Hause gelassen
      I've left it at home
   sie hat sich überreden lassen
      she allowed herself to be persuaded
   er hat sich einen Bart wachsen lassen
      he has grown a beard
   sonst hätte ich den Arzt kommen lassen
      otherwise I'd have got the doctor to come

-lein See DIMINUTIVES.

letter-writing In a letter to a friend the
usual greeting is:
   Lieber Dieter/Liebe Ingrid,
      Dear Dieter/Ingrid,
   Liebe Ingrid, lieber Dieter,
      Dear Ingrid and Dieter,
   If you are writing a business letter, or a more
formal letter, it is usual to start:
   Sehr geehrter Herr Teubert,
      Dear Mr Teubert,

Sehr geehrte Frau Pohl,
   Dear Mrs Pohl,
Sehr geehrte Herren,
   Dear Sir(s),
Sehr geehrte Damen und Herren,
   Dear Sir or Madam,
Use of an exclamation mark after the greeting is now considered old-fashioned.

The first word of the actual letter does not begin with a capital letter (unless, of course, it is a noun). Any translation of 'you' or 'your' in German is always written with a capital in letters, even when the 'du' or 'ihr' form is being used:

vielen Dank für Deinen Brief
   Thank you very much for your letter

The commonest ways of finishing an informal letter in German are:

(*to one friend*)
Es grüßt Dich
         Deine Barbara
or **Viele Grüße**
         Dein Reinhard
(*to more than one friend*)
Es grüßt Euch
         Euer Georg
or **Viele Grüße (an Euch beide/alle)**
         von Eurer Evi

The most common way of signing off a business letter or a more formal letter is simply:

Mit freundlichen Grüßen
Peter Strauch
See also ADDRESSES.

mal is often used as a 'filler word':
hör mal!
   listen
ich komm' mal vorbei
   I'll drop round
kannst du mir mal helfen?
   can you help me?

man is used to mean 'one', 'you', 'people in general', 'they' or 'somebody'.

nom	acc	gen	dat
man	einen	–	einem

man kann nie wissen
you (or one) never can tell
man hat mir das erklärt
somebody explained it to me
das kann einem weh tun
that can be painful
man sagt, ...
they or people say ...

'Man' is also used to express passive ideas:

man hat mir meine Brieftasche gestohlen
my wallet has been stolen

manch 1. In literary language, 'manch' is used without any endings at all to mean 'many a'. An adjective coming between it and the noun has the strong ADJECTIVE endings:

manch aufregendes Abenteuer
many a thrilling adventure

2. 'Manch' can also be used as an article (that is, instead of 'a' or 'the' before a noun), or as a pronoun. The declension is the same for both these uses:

	masc	sing fem	neut	pl all genders
nom	mancher	manche	manches	manche
acc	manchen	manche	manches	manche
gen	manches	mancher	manches	mancher
dat	manchem	mancher	manchem	manchen

article: **manche Leute**
many people
an manchen Stellen
in many places
pronoun: **das hat schon mancher gesagt**
many a person has said that before
manche glauben das
many people believe it

When it is used as an article in the singular, any

adjective coming between it and the noun has the weak ADJECTIVE endings:

> **manches heimliche Treffen**
> many a secret meeting

When it is used as an article in the plural, an adjective coming after it can have either the strong or the weak ADJECTIVE endings:

> **manche deutsche(n) Studenten**
> many German students

measurements and quantities

Masculine and neuter nouns used to express measurements and quantities are generally singular when they have a number in front of them; feminine nouns are generally plural:

> **Tageshöchsttemperatur zwanzig Grad**
> maximum temperature twenty degrees
> **vier Meter lang**
> four metres long
> **ich nehme fünf Stück**
> I'll take five (of them)
> **zwei Glas Wein**
> two glasses of wine
> **drei Tassen Kaffee**
> three cups of coffee

The noun coming after the expression of measurement or quantity is usually in the same case as the measurement or quantity itself:

> **ein Glas heißes Wasser**
> a glass of hot water
> **er gab mir eine Flasche guten Wein**
> he gave me a bottle of good wine

mehrere   can be used either as an article (that is, instead of 'a' or 'the' in front of a noun), or as a pronoun. It is always plural, and its declension is the same for both uses:

nom	mehrere
acc	mehrere
gen	mehrerer
dat	mehreren

article: **wir mußten mehrere Stunden warten**
  we had to wait several hours
pronoun: **mehrere von seinen Freunden**
  several of his friends
When 'mehrere' is used as an article, any
adjective coming between it and the noun has the
strong ADJECTIVE endings:
  mehrere lange Reisen
  several long journeys

mein my. See POSSESSIVES.

mich accusative of 'ich'. See PERSONAL
PRONOUNS.

mir dative of 'ich'. See PERSONAL PRONOUNS.

mit takes the dative. See PREPOSITIONS.

mit- a SEPARABLE PREFIX which either has the
meaning 'with us/them etc', or suggests
participation in some activity:
  mitkommen: kommst du auch mit?
  are you coming (with us) too?

modal verbs are a small set of verbs which
express possibility, desire, necessity, or
obligation, and which can be used with the
infinitive of another verb in much the same way
as auxiliary verbs can be. The modal verbs are:

dürfen	*be allowed to, may*
können	*can, be able to*
mögen	*may, might, like to*
müssen	*must, have to*
sollen	*ought to, should, be supposed to*
wollen	*want to*

When they are used with the infinitive of another
verb, that infinitive goes to the end of the clause.
'Zu' is not used:
  ich kann morgen leider nicht kommen
  unfortunately I can't (*or* won't be able to)
  come tomorrow
  das mag wohl sein that may well be

er wollte einfach nicht helfen
　he simply didn't want to help
The modal verbs are quite often used in the
subjunctive, either to express politeness, or to be
less definite:

wir möchten bitte zahlen
　could we have the bill, please?
könnten Sie mir vielleicht sagen, ...?
　could you please tell me ...?
ich müßte eigentlich jetzt gehen
　I really ought to go now
All the modal verbs have two forms of the past
participle. The 'ge...' form is only used if there is
no infinitive of another verb; when there is an
infinitive of another verb in the clause, the past
participle of the modal verb has the same form as
its infinitive:

sie hatte es schon immer so gewollt
　she had always wanted it like that
sie hatte es schon immer machen wollen
　she had always wanted to do it
ich werde heute nicht schlafen können
　I won't be able to sleep tonight

mögen is a MODAL VERB meaning 'may, might,
like to'. Its principle parts are:
　mögen, mag, mochte, gemocht/mögen
and it uses 'haben' as its auxiliary. The present
tense is irregular:

ich	mag	wir	mögen
du	magst	ihr	mögt
er, sie,		Sie	mögen
es	mag	sie	mögen

money Nouns referring to units of currency
are generally used in the singular in German
when they have a number in front of them:

drei Mark achtzig (DM3,80)
　three marks eighty (pfennigs)
das kostet zwanzig Schilling
　that costs twenty Austrian schillings

months of the year   are all masculine:

Januar	Juli
Februar	August
März	September
April	Oktober
Mai	November
Juni	Dezember

Except in one or two set phrases 'der' is usually used with the name of a month:

der April hat nur dreißig Tage
  there are only thirty days in April
im September
  in (*or* during) September
but: **Anfang/Ende März**
  at the beginning/end of March
See also DATES.

müssen   is a MODAL VERB meaning 'must, have to'. Its principle parts are:
  müssen, muß, mußte, gemußt/müssen
and it uses 'haben' as its auxiliary. The present tense is irregular:

ich	muß	*wir*	müssen
du	mußt	*ihr*	müßt
er, sie,		*Sie*	müssen
es	muß	*sie*	müssen

nach   takes the dative. See PREPOSITIONS.

nach-   is a SEPARABLE PREFIX which often has the idea of 'after' or 'later', or of copying someone:
  **nachkommen: geht voraus, ich komme
    nach** you go on ahead, I'll follow you
  **nachkaufen: kann ich sie nachkaufen,
    wenn ich noch welche brauche?** can I
    buy more later if I need them?
  nachmachen: sie macht mir alles nach
    she copies everything I do

neben · takes either the accusative or the dative, depending on whether it is expressing movement or not. See PREPOSITIONS.

....

negatives There are two main ways of
expressing a negative in a German sentence.
  1. 'not'+verb/adjective/adverb=**nicht**
In a clause with an intransitive verb, in which
the word order is that of a basic statement, 'nicht'
comes immediately after the verb (or immediately
after the auxiliary verb):
> **ich rauche nicht**
>   I don't smoke
> **sie ist nicht gerade hübsch**
>   she's not exactly pretty
> **nur Dieter hat nicht gelacht**
>   only Dieter didn't laugh

But if there is an object or an indirect object, or
if the subject comes after the verb, 'nicht' is
positioned as follows:
> **ich habe dich nicht gesehen**
>   I didn't see you
> **seien Sie nicht böse!**
>   don't be cross!
> **hat es euch nicht gefallen?**
>   didn't you like it?

'Nicht' can be made more emphatic by using
'gar' or 'überhaupt' in front of it ('überhaupt' is
slightly stronger):
> **das gefällt mir gar nicht** (*or* **überhaupt
> nicht**) I don't like that at all
> **ich darf gar nicht** (*or* **überhaupt nicht**)
> **daran denken**
>   it doesn't bear thinking about

  2. 'not'+noun=**kein**. See the entry at KEIN.
Like 'nicht', it can be made more emphatic by
using 'gar' or 'überhaupt' with it:
> **ich habe gar kein** (*or* **überhaupt kein**)
> **Geld** I've no money at all

nicht 1. not. See NEGATIVES I.
  2. **nicht wahr?** is used to mean 'doesn't it?',
'isn't he?', 'wasn't she?', 'will it?' etc, tagged onto
the end of a sentence. It is much more informal to
leave off the 'wahr', but otherwise the two forms

are interchangeable:

Sie arbeiten doch bei Blohm, nicht wahr?
you work at Blohm's, don't you?
See also ODER.

nichts nothing. 'Nichts' never has any
endings no matter what case it is. It can be given
extra emphasis by using 'gar' or 'überhaupt'
before it:

sonst hat er nichts gemacht
apart from that he didn't do anything
nichts, was ich sage, ...
nothing that I say ...
sie hat gar nichts (*or* **überhaupt nichts**)
gesagt she didn't say anything at all
'Nichts' can be followed by an adjective used as
a noun. The adjective is written with a capital
letter and has the strong neuter endings:

**wenn Sie nichts Besseres vorschlagen
können** if you can't suggest anything
better

nieder- a SEPARABLE PREFIX meaning 'down':
**niederlassen: sie hatte sich in Berlin
niedergelassen** she had settled (down) in
Berlin

niemand nobody, not anybody. 'Niemand'
may be — but does not have to be — declined. The
exception is the genitive:

nom	niemand
acc	niemand(en)
gen	niemand(e)s
dat	niemand(em)

es war niemand da
there was nobody there
ich habe niemand(en) gesehen
I didn't see anybody
When it is followed by 'ander(e)s', it never has
any ending:

ich habe niemand ander(e)s getroffen
I didn't meet anybody else

nominative The nominative is used:
1. for the subject of the verb.
2. for the complement of 'sein', 'werden' and 'bleiben', and of 'heißen' when it means 'to be called':

> **er ist *ein berühmter Komponist***
>> he's a famous composer
>
> **das wird bestimmt *ein guter Urlaub***
>> I'm sure it's going to be a good holiday
>
> **Friedrich II. heißt oft *Friedrich der Große*** Frederick the Second is often called Frederick the Great

nouns There are three genders of nouns in German – masculine, feminine, and neuter – and each has a singular and a plural form. See GENDERS and PLURALS.

All German nouns decline, their declension depending largely on their gender.

◆I *Masculine*
Masculine nouns fall into three groups as regards declension – strong, weak, and mixed.

a) The strong nouns are by far the largest group. In the genitive singular they add **-s** if they end in **-el**, **-em**, **-en**, **-er** or **-ling**, or are colours or languages; **-es** if they end in **-s**, **-ß**, **-z**, **-sch** or **-st**; in all other cases either **-s** or **-es** may be used. In the dative singular they may optionally add **-e** if they do not end in **-el**, **-em**, **-en**, **-er** or a vowel. In the dative plural they add **-n** to their plural form if this does not already end in **-n**.

b) The weak nouns add **-en** (or **-n** if they end in **-e** or **-er**) in all the singular cases except the nominative. They also form their plural with **-en**, and no other ending is added in any plural case. The group of weak nouns includes:
– all masculine nouns ending in **-e**, including nationalities;
– virtually all nouns ending in **-and**, **-ant**, **-ent**, **-graph**, **-ist**, **-krat**, **-nom** or **-oge**;

– the following common nouns:

Bär	bear	Herr (+n)	Mr, lord
Bauer	farmer	Kamerad	comrade
Christ	Christian	Mensch	person
Elefant	elephant	Nachbar (+n)	neighbour
Fürst	prince	Narr	fool
Graf	count	Prinz	prince
Held	hero	Soldat	soldier

c) The mixed nouns are a very small group. They add -**ns** in the genitive singular and -**n** in the accusative and dative singular. Their plurals are also formed by adding -**n**:

Buchstabe	letter	Glaube	belief
Funke	spark	Name	name
Gedanke	thought	Wille	will

The endings of the masculine declensions are:

strong

	sing		pl	
nom	der	—	die	-(pl)-
acc	den	—	die	-(pl)-
gen	des	-(e)s	der	-(pl)-
dat	dem	-(e)	den	-(pl)-n

weak

nom	der	—	die	-(e)n
acc	den	-(e)n	die	-(e)n
gen	des	-(e)n	der	-(e)n
dat	dem	-(e)n	den	-(e)n

mixed

nom	der	—	die	-n
acc	den	-n	die	-n
gen	des	-ns	der	-n
dat	dem	-n	den	-n

◆II *Feminine*

Feminine nouns do not change at all in any of the singular cases. If their plural form does not already end in -**n**, they add -**n** in the dative plural:

	sing		pl	
nom	die	—	die	-(pl)-
acc	die	—	die	-(pl)-
gen	der	—	der	-(pl)-
dat	der	—	den	-(pl)-n

....

◆III *Neuter*

Neuter nouns all behave in the same way as strong masculine nouns, with the exception of 'das Herz' and words like 'das Kino', 'das Foto' etc.

		sing			*pl*
nom	das	—	die	-(pl)-	
acc	das	—	die	-(pl)-	
gen	des	-(e)s	der	-(pl)-	
dat	dem	-(e)	den	-(pl)-n	

nom	das	Herz	die	Herzen	
acc	das	Herz	die	Herzen	
gen	des	Herzens	der	Herzen	
dat	dem	Herzen	den	Herzen	

For information on case usage see NOMINATIVE, ACCUSATIVE, GENITIVE and DATIVE.

number By the 'number' of a word is meant the state of being singular or plural.

numbers ◆I *Cardinal numbers (one, two, three, etc)*

0	null	20	zwanzig
1	eins	21	einundzwanzig
2	zwei (*or* zwo)	22	zweiundzwanzig
3	drei	23	dreiundzwanzig
4	vier	24	vierundzwanzig
5	fünf	25	fünfundzwanzig
6	sechs	26	sechsundzwanzig
7	sieben	27	siebenundzwanzig
8	acht	28	achtundzwanzig
9	neun	29	neunundzwanzig
10	zehn	30	dreißig
11	elf	31	einunddreißig
12	zwölf	40	vierzig
13	dreizehn	50	fünfzig
14	vierzehn	60	sechzig
15	fünfzehn	70	siebzig
16	sechzehn	80	achtzig
17	siebzehn	90	neunzig
18	achtzehn	100	hundert
19	neunzehn	101	hunderteins

175	hundertfünfundsiebzig
200	zweihundert
1,000	tausend, 1.000
1,001	tausendeins, 1.001
1,100	tausendeinhundert, 1.100
2,000	zweitausend, 2.000
1,000,000	eine Million, 1.000.000
1,000,000,000	eine Milliarde, 1.000.000.000

Although in counting 'eins' is used for 'one', in front of a noun the indefinite article **ein** is used instead:

mit einer Hand with one hand

'Zwo' can be used instead of 'zwei' to avoid confusion with 'drei'.

In German, either a full stop or a space is used to separate off the thousands.

◆II *Ordinal numbers (first, second, etc)*

1st	(der, die, das) erste, 1.	11th	elfte, 11.
2nd	zweite, 2.	12th	zwölfte, 12.
3rd	dritte, 3.	13th	dreizehnte, 13.
4th	vierte, 4.	14th	vierzehnte, 14.
5th	fünfte, 5.	15th	fünfzehnte, 15.
6th	sechste, 6.	16th	sechzehnte, 16.
7th	siebte, 7.	17th	siebzehnte, 17.
8th	achte, 8.	18th	achtzehnte, 18.
9th	neunte, 9.	19th	neunzehnte, 19.
10th	zehnte, 10.	20th	zwanzigste, 20.

Any other ordinal number can be formed simply by adding **-ste** to the cardinal number.

All ordinal numbers are adjectives and decline.

◆III *Fractions*

$\frac{1}{5}$	*ein Fünftel*	$\frac{3}{5}$	*drei Fünftel*
$\frac{1}{4}$	*ein Viertel*	$\frac{3}{4}$	*Dreiviertel*
$\frac{1}{3}$	*ein Drittel*	$1\frac{1}{4}$	*eineinviertel*
$\frac{1}{2}$	*ein halb*	$1\frac{1}{2}$	*anderthalb, eineinhalb*
$\frac{2}{3}$	*zwei Drittel*	$2\frac{1}{2}$	*zweineinhalb*

'Die Hälfte' is used mainly to refer to half of a group of things or people, or when there is no noun following; if there is a following noun which does not refer to a group of things or people, the

adjective **halb** is more common:
> **ich habe nur die Hälfte (davon) gelesen**
>> I've only read half of them
> **die halbe Stadt**
>> half the town
> **halb München**
>> half Munich
> **vor einer halben Stunde**
>> half an hour ago

◆IV *Decimals*
   0.2   null Komma zwei,   0,2
   1.33   eins Komma dreiunddreißig,   1,33

ob 1. whether. 'Ob' is a CONJUNCTION that affects the word order of the sentence.
   2. 'Ob' is often used at the beginning of a question that you have asked before but have to repeat because it has not been heard:
> **kommt sie mit? – was? – ob sie mitkommt**
>> is she coming too? – what? – (I said,) is she coming too?

   3. 'Und ob' is often used in informal German as an emphatic answer to a question:
> **hast du es gesehen? – und ob!**
>> did you see it? – you bet!

obgleich, obschon, obwohl   are CONJUNCTIONS which affect the word order of the sentence. They all mean 'although', but 'obschon' is less common.

object case   See ACCUSATIVE.

oder 1. or. 'Oder' is a CONJUNCTION which does not affect the word order of the sentence.
   2. 'Oder?' is used to mean 'isn't he?', 'wasn't she?', 'will it?' etc, tagged onto the end of a sentence when the speaker wants confirmation:
> **du kommst doch auch mit, oder?**
>> you're coming too, aren't you?
> **das paßt bestimmt nicht, oder?**
>> surely that won't fit, will it?

ohne without. 'Ohne' is a PREPOSITION that takes the accusative, but when it is used to mean 'without . . . ing' it takes zu and an infinitive:

ohne mich zu fragen without asking me

paar: ein paar, meaning 'a few', always has the same form no matter what case it is:

wir bleiben noch ein paar Minuten
we'll stay a few more minutes

participles See PAST PARTICIPLE and PRESENT PARTICIPLE.

parts of the body When talking about parts of the body in the following sorts of construction in German it is usual to use the dative of the personal pronoun instead of the possessive adjective:

ich muß mir die Haare waschen
I must wash my hair
er flüsterte mir ins Ohr
he whispered in my ear

passive The passive in German is formed by using WERDEN and the past participle of the verb. There is a complete set of passive tenses.
Present=*I am (being) beaten*
  ich werde geschlagen
Imperfect=*I was (being) beaten*
  ich wurde geschlagen
Perfect=*I was (or have been) beaten*
  ich bin geschlagen worden
Pluperfect=*I had been beaten*
  ich war geschlagen worden
Future=*I will be beaten*
  ich werde geschlagen werden
Future Perfect=*I will have been beaten*
  ich werde geschlagen worden sein
Conditional=*I would be beaten*
  ich würde geschlagen werden
Conditional Perfect=*I would have been beaten*
  ich würde geschlagen worden sein

....

Von+dative is used for the human agent carrying out an action, and **durch**+accusative for the inanimate cause of an action:

> **Elke wurde von ihrer Mutter/durch den Lärm geweckt** Elke was woken by her mother/by the noise

The passive can also be expressed with MAN.

past participle See VERBS and IRREGULAR VERBS.

The German past participle can be used as an adjective, with the ordinary adjective endings:

> **die noch nicht angekommenen Pakete** the parcels that haven't yet arrived

perfect tense This corresponds in English to 'I played', 'I have played', 'I have been playing', and 'I did play':

> **als ich jung war, habe ich öfter Tennis gespielt** when I was young I played tennis quite often
>
> **ich habe noch nie Tennis gespielt** I've never played tennis
>
> **ich habe gerade Tennis gespielt** I've just been playing tennis
>
> **das stimmt, ich habe wirklich mit ihm Tennis gespielt** that's right, I did play tennis with him

The perfect tense is very often used in conversation in preference to the imperfect tense. See also VERBS and PRESENT TENSE 2.

personal pronouns

	nom		acc	gen	dat
sing	ich	*I*	mich	meiner	mir
	du	*you*	dich	deiner	dir
	er	*(he)*	ihn	seiner	ihm
	sie	*(she)*	sie	ihrer	ihr
	es	*(it)*	es	seiner	ihm
pl	wir	*we*	uns	unserer	uns
	ihr	*you*	euch	eurer	euch
	Sie	*you*	Sie	Ihrer	Ihnen
	sie	*they*	sie	ihrer	ihnen

1. 'Du, dich, deiner, dir' is used to address members of the family, friends, and children up to their mid-teens. This form of address is also used quite often among young people, especially in student circles, even when they have not met each other before. The related plural is 'ihr, euch, eurer, euch'. See also LETTER-WRITING.

The polite form of 'you' is 'Sie, Sie, Ihrer, Ihnen'. It is always written with a capital letter, and always takes a plural verb even when it refers to only one person.

2. The use of 'er', 'sie' and 'es' does not correspond to 'he', 'she', 'it' in that the gender of the pronoun is grammatical in German rather than factual; it is determined purely by the gender of the noun it replaces:

ein Mädchen ... *es* hatte lange Haare
a girl ... she had long hair
mein Schlüssel ... ich finde *ihn* nicht
my key ... I can't find it

3. In the 3rd person genitive, 'seiner' and 'ihrer' are replaced by 'dessen' (masculine and neuter singular) and 'deren' (feminine singular and all plurals) when they refer to things rather than people:

ich schäme mich seiner*/dessen
I am ashamed of him/it
*this usage is rare or literary.

4. With most prepositions DA- (or DAR- before vowels) is used instead of the 3rd person pronoun when referring to things rather than people:

ich interessiere mich nicht für ihn/dafür
I'm not interested in him/in it
davon habe ich wenig verstanden
I didn't understand much of it

However, 'da(r)-' is not used if there is a relative pronoun following:

**von dem, was er sagte, habe ich wenig
verstanden** I didn't understand much of
what he said

place names   As a general rule, most towns
and cities are neuter in gender, although the
gender is really only important when an adjective
is used with the place name:

das ewige Rom
Rome, the eternal city

An adjective can be made from the name of a
town or city by adding **-er**. Such adjectives never
decline.

der Regensburger Dom
Regensburg cathedral

das stand in einer Berliner Zeitung
it was in a Berlin newspaper

See also COUNTRIES.

pluperfect tense   This corresponds in
English to either 'I had laughed' or 'I had been
laughing':

früher hatte er darüber gelacht
he had laughed about it earlier, he had
been laughing about it earlier

See also VERBS and IMPERFECT TENSE 2.

plurals   1. Masculine
Most masculine nouns of one syllable, whose
vowel is **-i-** or **-e-** (or both), add **-e**:

| der Tisch | *table* | die Tische |
| der Brief | *letter* | die Briefe |

If they contain an **-a-**, **-o-** or **-u-**, they generally
add **-̈e**:

der Ball	*ball*	die Bälle
der Baum	*tree*	die Bäume
der Sohn	*son*	die Söhne
der Hut	*hat*	die Hüte

but there are some common exceptions which
simply add **-e**:

der Arm	*arm*	die Arme
der Dom	*cathedral*	die Dome
der Hund	*dog*	die Hunde
der Ort	*place*	die Orte
der Pfad	*path*	die Pfade

der Ruf	*call*	die Rufe
der Schuh	*shoe*	die Schuhe
der Stoff	*fabric*	die Stoffe
der Tag	*day*	die Tage

Most masculine nouns ending in **-el, -en** or **-er** have the same form in the plural as they have in the singular:

der Hügel	*hill*	die Hügel
der Kuchen	*cake*	die Kuchen
der Fahrer	*driver*	die Fahrer

Some add an umlaut in the plural. The most common of these are:

der Apfel	*apple*	die Äpfel
der Bruder	*brother*	die Brüder
der Garten	*garden*	die Gärten
der Hafen	*harbour*	die Häfen
der Hammer	*hammer*	die Hämmer
der Kasten	*box*	die Kästen
der Laden	*shop*	die Läden
der Mangel	*lack*	die Mängel
der Nagel	*nail*	die Nägel
der Ofen	*stove*	die Öfen
der Schaden	*damage*	die Schäden
der Schwager	*brother-in-law*	die Schwäger
der Vater	*father*	die Väter
der Vogel	*bird*	die Vögel

A small number of masculine nouns add **-er** in the plural. The only two common ones are:

der Geist	*spirit*	die Geister
der Leib	*body*	die Leiber

A few nouns add **⁝er**, the most common ones being:

der Gott	*god*	die Götter
der Irrtum	*mistake*	die Irrtümer
der Mann	*man, husband*	die Männer
der Mund	*mouth*	die Münder
der Rand	*edge*	die Ränder
der Reichtum	*fortune*	die Reichtümer
der Strauch	*bush*	die Sträucher

....

| der Wald | *forest* | die Wälder |
| der Wurm | *worm* | die Würmer |

Some masculine nouns add **-en** in the plural (or **-n** if they end in **-e** or **-er**). This group includes the weak and mixed nouns (see NOUNS I), nouns ending in **-or**, and the following nouns:

der Schmerz	*pain*	die Schmerzen
der See	*lake*	die Seen
der Staat	*state*	die Staaten
der Strahl	*ray*	die Strahlen
der Vetter	*cousin*	die Vettern

The following masculine nouns have regular plurals:

sing	*pl*	*sing*	*pl*
-ar	-are	-ig	-ige
-är	-äre	-ling	-linge
-eur	-eure	-or	-oren
-ich	-iche		

2. Feminine

Most feminine nouns form their plural by adding **-en** (or **-n** if they end in **-e**, **-er** or **-el**):

die Uhr	*clock*	die Uhren
die Gabel	*fork*	die Gabeln
die Krankheit	*illness*	die Krankheiten
die Fähigkeit	*ability*	die Fähigkeiten
die Gesellschaft	*company*	die Gesellschaften
die Universität	*university*	die Universitäten
die Hoffnung	*hope*	die Hoffnungen

Some feminine nouns add ⁼e in the plural. The most common of these are:

die Angst	*fear*	die Ängste
die Auskunft	*information*	die Auskünfte
die Axt	*axe*	die Äxte
die Bank*	*bench*	die Bänke
die Braut	*bride*	die Bräute
die Brust	*breast*	die Brüste
die Faust	*fist*	die Fäuste
die Frucht	*fruit*	die Früchte
die Gans	*goose*	die Gänse
die Hand	*hand*	die Hände

die Haut	*skin*	die Häute
die Kraft	*strength*	die Kräfte
die Kuh	*cow*	die Kühe
die Kunst	*art*	die Künste
die Luft	*air*	die Lüfte
die Macht	*power*	die Mächte
die Maus	*mouse*	die Mäuse
die Nacht	*night*	die Nächte
die Naht	*seam*	die Nähte
die Not	*need*	die Nöte
die Nuß	*nut*	die Nüsse
die Schnur	*string*	die Schnüre
die Stadt	*town*	die Städte
die Wand	*wall*	die Wände
die Wurst	*sausage*	die Würste

*'die Bank' meaning 'bank' has the plural 'die Banken'.

There are only two feminine nouns which form the plural simply by adding an umlaut:

| die Mutter | *mother* | die Mütter |
| die Tochter | *daughter* | die Töchter |

Feminine nouns ending in **-in** add **-nen**:

| die Ärztin | *doctor* | die Ärztinnen |

3. Neuter

All neuter nouns ending in **-chen** or **-lein**, and most ending in **-el**, **-en** or **-er** have the same form in the plural as in the singular:

das Mädchen	*girl*	die Mädchen
das Segel	*sail*	die Segel
das Messer	*knife*	die Messer
das Zeichen	*sign*	die Zeichen

A large number of neuter nouns add **-er** in the plural, or **-̈er** if they contain an **-a-**, **-o-** or **-u-**:

das Blatt	*leaf*	die Blätter
das Brett	*board*	die Bretter
das Buch	*book*	die Bücher
das Dorf	*village*	die Dörfer
das Ei	*egg*	die Eier
das Haus	*house*	die Häuser
das Kind	*child*	die Kinder

Another large group of neuter nouns add -e in the plural:

das Argument	argument	die Argumente
das Bein	leg	die Beine
das Ding	thing	die Dinge
das Haar	hair	die Haare
das Öl	oil	die Öle
das Paket	packet	die Pakete

A smaller number of neuter nouns add -en in the plural (or -n if they already end in -e):

das Auge	eye	die Augen
das Bett	bed	die Betten
das Ende	end	die Enden
das Hemd	shirt	die Hemden
das Insekt	insect	die Insekten
das Interesse	interest	die Interessen
das Leid	sorrow	die Leiden
das Ohr	ear	die Ohren

Neuter nouns ending in -nis add -se:

das Erlebnis	experience	die Erlebnisse
das Geheimnis	secret	die Geheimnisse

Neuter nouns ending in -ium form their plural in -ien, and some ending in -um form their plural with -en:

das Gremium	committee	die Gremien
das Gymnasium	grammar school	die Gymnasien
das Zentrum	centre	die Zentren

A few neuter nouns which were originally foreign words add -s in the plural:

das Auto	car	die Autos
das Büro	office	die Büros
das Café	café	die Cafés
das Hotel	hotel	die Hotels
das Kino	cinema	die Kinos
das Kotelett	chop	die Koteletts
das Radio	radio	die Radios
das Restaurant	restaurant	die Restaurants
das Sofa	sofa	die Sofas
das Taxi	taxi	die Taxis

4. Foreign words (loan words) and abbreviations add -s in the plural:

| der Song | *song* | die Songs |
| der BMW | *BMW* | die BMWs |

5. Notice also:

der Fachmann	*expert*	die Fachleute
der Geschäfts-	*business-*	die Geschäfts-
mann	*man*	leute

possessive case   See GENITIVE.

possessives   ◆I *Possessive adjectives*

These are the equivalents of 'my', 'your' etc.

| | *sing* | | | *pl* |
	masc	fem	neut	all genders
ich	mein	meine	mein	meine
du	dein	deine	dein	deine
er	sein	seine	sein	seine
sie	ihr	ihre	ihr	ihre
es	sein	seine	sein	seine
wir	unser	uns(e)re	unser	uns(e)re
ihr	euer	eure	euer	eure
Sie	Ihr	Ihre	Ihr	Ihre
sie	ihr	ihre	ihr	ihre

They decline like EIN and KEIN. Adjectives coming after them have the mixed ADJECTIVE endings.

◆II *Possessive pronouns*

These are the equivalents of 'mine', 'yours', 'theirs' etc. There are three forms of the possessive pronoun in German; they all have exactly the same meaning.

ich	1.	meiner, meine, mein(e)s; (*pl*) meine
	2.	der/die/das meine; (*pl*) die meinen
	3.	der/die/das meinige; (*pl*) die meinigen
du	1.	deiner, deine, dein(e)s; (*pl*) deine
	2.	der/die/das deine; (*pl*) die deinen
	3.	der/die/das deinige; (*pl*) die deinigen
er	1.	seiner, seine, sein(e)s; (*pl*) seine
	2.	der/die/das seine; (*pl*) die seinen
	3.	der/die/das seinige; (*pl*) die seinigen

....

sie	1.	ihrer, ihre, ihr(e)s; (*pl*) ihre
	2.	der/die/das ihre; (*pl*) die ihren
	3.	der/die/das ihrige; (*pl*) die ihrigen
es	1.	seiner, seine, sein(e)s; (*pl*) seine
	2.	der/die/das seine; (*pl*) die seinen
	3.	der/die/das seinige; (*pl*) die seinigen
wir	1.	uns(e)rer, uns(e)re, uns(e)res; (*pl*) uns(e)re
	2.	der/die/das uns(e)re; (*pl*) die uns(e)ren
	3.	der/die/das uns(e)rige; (*pl*) die uns(e)rigen
ihr	1.	eurer, eure, eures; (*pl*) eure
	2.	der/die/das eure; (*pl*) die euren
	3.	der/die/das eurige; (*pl*) die eurigen
Sie	1.	Ihrer, Ihre, Ihr(e)s; (*pl*) Ihre
	2.	der/die/das Ihre; (*pl*) die Ihren
	3.	der/die/das Ihrige; (*pl*) die Ihrigen
sie	1.	ihrer, ihre, ihr(e)s; (*pl*) ihre
	2.	der/die/das ihre; (*pl*) die ihren
	3.	der/die/das ihrige; (*pl*) die ihrigen

The first form is declined like DIESER, DIESE, DIESES. The second and third forms are declined like DER, DIE, DAS followed by an adjective (with the weak endings).

predicative An adjective is used predicatively when it comes after a verb, and not before a noun.

prepositions fall into four groups, according to the case that is used with them:
1. accusative:

bis	*as far as, up to, until, by*
durch	*through, by*
für	*for*
gegen	*against, towards*
ohne	*without*
um	*around, at*

2. dative:

aus	*out of, from*

außer	*except for*
bei	*at, near*
dank*	*thanks to*
entgegen	*against*
gegenüber	*opposite*
gemäß	*according to*
mit	*with*
nach	*towards, after, according to*
seit	*since*
von	*from, of, by*
zu	*to*

*can also take the genitive

'Entgegen', 'gemäß' and 'nach' can come after the noun rather than before it. 'Gegenüber' comes after pronouns.

3. accusative or dative:

an	*on (vertical), at, to*
auf	*on (horizontal)*
hinter	*behind*
in	*into, in*
neben	*near, next to, beside*
über	*over, above, across*
unter	*under, among*
vor	*in front of, before*
zwischen	*between*

The accusative expresses movement to or from a place, and the dative expresses rest or movement within a place:

sie legte die Bücher auf den Tisch
   she put the books on the table
die Bücher lagen auf dem Tisch
   the books were lying on the table
sie gingen in den Garten hinaus
   they went out into the garden
sie liefen im Garten herum
   they were running around in the garden

Entlang meaning 'along' or 'along the side of' has the following uses:

er fuhr die Straße entlang
   he drove along the road

....

wir sind am Fluß entlang (*or* **den Fluß
entlang**) **spaziert** we walked along the
river

die Bäume stehen entlang dem Weg (*or*
entlang des Weges) the trees stand
along(side) the path

4. genitive:

anhand	*by means of*
(an)statt	*instead of*
aufgrund	*because of*
außerhalb	*outside*
diesseits	*this side of*
innerhalb	*inside*
jenseits	*on the other side of*
kraft	*by virtue of*
mittels	*by means of*
oberhalb	*above*
trotz*	*in spite of*
um ... willen	*for the sake of*
unterhalb	*below*
während	*during*
wegen*	*because of*

*can also take the dative.

There are also special forms of PERSONAL
PRONOUNS, RELATIVE PRONOUNS and
INTERROGATIVE WORDS which combine with most
prepositions to form one-word contractions:

die Hälfte davon half of it

etwas, worauf ich mich freue
something that I'm looking forward to

woher wissen Sie das?
how do you know that?

present participle   See -ING FORMS.

In German the present participle is formed by
adding **-d** to the infinitive. It can only be used as
an adjective in front of a noun or as an adverb:

die zu streichenden Ziffern
the figures to be deleted

sie kam lachend ins Zimmer
she came into the room laughing

present tense 1. This corresponds in English to 'I speak', 'I am speaking', 'I do speak', 'I am going to speak', and 'I will speak':

> **sie spricht sehr deutlich**
> she speaks very clearly

> **sie spricht gerade davon**
> she's talking about it now

> **doch, sie spricht Deutsch**
> yes she does speak German

> **und wenn wir sie nicht verstehen, spricht sie dann Englisch?** and if we don't understand, will she speak English?

See the entry VERBS.

2. Note the following use of the present tense in German:

> **wie lange arbeitest du schon bei der Firma?** how long have you been working with that company?

> **er wohnt schon seit drei Jahren hier** he has lived here for three years

pronouns The number and gender of a pronoun on any one occasion depend on the number and gender of the noun that it replaces. The case, however, depends on the function that the pronoun itself has in the sentence:

> **mein Kuli ist verschwunden – hast du *einen*?** my biro's disappeared – have you got one?

> **das Mädchen, *das*...**
> the girl (that *or* who)...

See PERSONAL PRONOUNS, POSSESSIVES, REFLEXIVE PRONOUNS, and RELATIVE PRONOUNS.

punctuation See COLONS, COMMAS, FULL STOPS etc.

questions 1. Questions are formed by inverting the subject and the verb (or auxiliary verb):

> **kommst du mit?**
> are you coming with us?

kennen Sie Frau Müller?
  do you know Frau Müller?
hat Hans Sabine eingeladen?
  has Hans invited Sabine?
wer hat dir das erzählt?
  who told you that?
was für ein Auto hat sie gekauft?
  what sort of car did she buy?
  2. Questions can also be formed in German by
tagging 'NICHT wahr' or ODER onto the end of a
statement.

ran, rauf, raus = heran, herauf, heraus.
See HER-.

reflexive pronouns   These are the
equivalents of 'myself', 'yourself' etc. They are
only used in the accusative and dative, and agree
with the subject of the sentence:

	acc	dat
ich	mich	mir
du	dich	dir
er, sie, es	sich	sich
wir	uns	uns
ihr	euch	euch
Sie	sich	sich
sie	sich	sich

Reflexive pronouns can be used:
1. with verbs:
   hast du dich verletzt?
     have you hurt yourself?
   wasch dir schnell mal die Hände
     wash your hands quickly
2. with prepositions:
   ich hatte den Brief bei mir
     I had the letter on me
3. to mean 'each other':
   wir schreiben uns regelmäßig
     we write to each other regularly
   sie begegneten sich vor dem Gericht
     they met (each other) in court

reflexive verbs fall into two main groups.

1. With the first group, the REFLEXIVE PRONOUN is just an ordinary direct or indirect object of the verb:

er hat sich (*acc*) **umgebracht**
he killed himself

ich ziehe mich schnell an
I'll just get dressed

sie hat sich (*dat*) **ein neues Auto gekauft**
she's bought herself a new car

hol dir einen Stuhl!
fetch yourself a chair

2. With verbs in the second group, however, the reflexive pronoun is an essential part of the verb. The English translation of these verbs very rarely includes 'myself', 'herself' etc, so the reflexive pronoun should be learnt as a part of the verb. In this group, the reflexive pronoun is always in the accusative unless the verb can also have a direct object; if it can have a direct object the reflexive pronoun is in the dative:

ich muß mich beeilen
I must hurry

warum hast du dich entschlossen, Anglistik zu studieren? why did you decide to study English?

das kann ich mir nicht leisten
I can't afford that

das hättest du dir vorher überlegen müssen!
you should have thought about that before

regular verbs in German are often called 'weak verbs'. See section I of the entry VERBS.

rein = herein. See HER-.

relative clauses are a type of SUBORDINATE CLAUSE. In English they begin with 'who', 'which', or 'that'; in German they usually begin with 'der, die, das', and they are always separated off from the rest of the sentence with commas.

....

relative pronouns introduce subordinate
clauses; any clause with a relative pronoun
should be separated off with commas and have its
verb at the end. The most commonly used relative
pronoun is DER, DIE, DAS. This has the same
number and gender as the noun it refers back to,
but its case depends on the function it has in its
own clause. It can never be omitted in German in
the way in which 'that' can be in English:

>**das Mädchen, *das* mir gegenüber saß**
>the girl (who was) sitting opposite me

>**der Junge, *den* ich gestern kennenlernte,
>ist ihr Bruder** the boy (that) I met
>yesterday is her brother

>**die Leute, bei *denen* ich wohne**
>the people I live with

WELCHER, WELCHE, WELCHES is normally only
used as a means of avoiding ugly repetition:

>**die, welche die Wohnung gekauft hat**
>the lady who bought the flat

The relative pronoun WAS should be used in the
following cases:

1. to refer back to 'das', 'dasselbe', 'alles',
'einiges', 'etwas', 'manches', 'nichts' or 'vieles':

>**das, was du sagst, stimmt nicht genau**
>what you are saying isn't quite right

>**alles, was ich besitze, gehört auch dir**
>everything I have belongs to you too

2. to refer back to an adjective used as a noun:

>**das Komischste, was ich je gehört habe**
>the funniest thing I've ever heard

3. to refer back to a whole clause:

>**er wollte nicht mitkommen, was sie
>einfach nicht verstehen konnte**
>he didn't want to come, which was
>something she just couldn't understand

4. if there is nothing to refer back to:

>**mach, was du denkst**
>do what you like

If in any of the above cases a preposition occurs
with the relative pronoun, a combining form wo-
(or wor- if the preposition begins with a vowel)
can be used instead:

> **er hat mir vieles erzählt, wovon (*or* von
> dem) ich nur wenig geglaubt habe**
> he told me a great deal, of which I only
> believed a little

> **das Buch, auf dem (*or* auf welchem *or*
> worauf) die Vase stand** the book the vase
> was standing on

The relative pronoun wo on its own is only used
if the noun that is referred back to is a noun of
place or time. DA can also be used to refer to time,
but it is not very common:

> **in der Stadt, wo ich wohne**
> in the town where I live

> **in den Tagen, wo (*or* da) alle noch ärmer
> waren**
> in the days when everyone was poorer

WER is used when the relative clause comes
before the main clause:

> **wer das gemacht hat, der soll sich melden**
> the person who did that should come
> forward

> **wer viel liest, (der) lernt auch viel**
> people who read a lot also learn a lot

5. when a relative pronoun is used to refer to a
personal pronoun then that personal pronoun
must be repeated:

> **wir, die *wir* immer bestrebt sind, ...**
> we who are always striving ...

rüber =herüber. See HER-.

runter =herunter. See HER-.

sein has two functions – it is one of the
AUXILIARY VERBS, and it can also be used as the
main verb in the sentence, followed by either an
adjective or by a noun in the nominative. Its
principle parts are:

....

sein, ist, war, gewesen
and it uses 'sein' as its auxiliary.

	present tense	*present subjunctive*
ich	bin	sei
du	bist	sei(e)st*
er, sie, es	ist	sei
wir	sind	seien
ihr	seid	seiet (*rare*)
Sie	sind	seien
sie	sind	seien
	imperfect tense	*imperfect subjunctive*
ich	war	wäre
du	warst	wär(e)st
er, sie, es	war	wäre
wir	waren	wären
ihr	wart	wär(e)t*
Sie	waren	wären
sie	waren	wären

perfect tense
   ich bin gewesen *etc*
imperative
   ('*du*' form) sei
   ('*ihr*' form) seid
   ('*Sie*' form) seien Sie
*The form with the 'e' is literary.

sein, seine, sein his, its, her. See
POSSESSIVES.

seit takes the dative. See PREPOSITIONS.

selber = SELBST. 'Selber' never changes its
form and never has any endings.

selbst myself, yourself, itself, themselves etc.
'Selbst' is used only for extra emphasis; it cannot
be used instead of a REFLEXIVE PRONOUN:
   ich selbst I myself
   das haben Sie selbst gesagt
      you said it yourself

'Selber' can always be used instead of 'selbst',
but it tends to be slightly more informal and
therefore not used very much in written German:

das glaubst du doch selbst (*or* **selber**)
nicht you don't even believe that yourself
das versteht sich von selbst
that's self-evident

separable prefixes
are prefixes which
are put at the front of the infinitive form of a verb,
but which are usually split off from the verb in all
its other forms.

When the verb is in the present tense or the
imperfect tense, in sentences with the word order
'subject – verb – rest of sentence', the prefix is split
off from the verb and put right at the end of the
sentence:

wegfahren: wir fahren morgen weg
we're going away tomorrow

The prefix is also put right at the end in
questions:

mitkommen: kommst du mit?
are you coming with us?

But when the verb has been sent to the end of a
SUBORDINATE CLAUSE, the prefix and the verb are
not split:

eintreten: als sie ins Zimmer eintrat
when she went into the room

To form the PAST PARTICIPLE of a verb with a
separable prefix, **-ge-** is inserted between the
prefix and the verb, and the usual past participle
ending is added to the end of the verb stem:

absagen – abgesagt
call off – called off
aussteigen – ausgestiegen
get out – got out

sich   is the REFLEXIVE PRONOUN related to 'er,
sie, es', 'sie' (*pl*), and 'Sie' (*polite 'you'*).

sie   she, it; they; her; them. See PERSONAL
PRONOUNS.

....

Sie is the polite form of 'you'. See PERSONAL PRONOUNS.

solch is used as an adjective and takes the weak, strong or mixed ADJECTIVE endings:

ein solcher Mensch a person like that

ich habe einen solchen Hunger
I'm so hungry

es gibt ja Leute, die solche Sachen mögen
there are people who like that kind of thing

Any adjective coming between it and the noun has the weak adjective endings:

bei solchem herrlichen Wetter
in such lovely weather

'Solch' can also be used in front of 'ein, eine, ein' or in front of another adjective without any ending at all. The other adjective has the strong adjective endings:

solch ein Mensch a person like that

bei solch herrlichem Wetter
in such lovely weather

sollen is a MODAL VERB meaning 'ought to, should, be supposed to'. Its principle parts are:

sollen, soll, sollte, gesollt/sollen

and it uses 'haben' as its auxiliary. The present tense is irregular:

ich	soll	*wir*	sollen
du	sollst	*ihr*	sollt
er, sie,		*Sie*	sollen
es	soll	*sie*	sollen

Note also the following use of **sollen**:

er soll ein guter Pianist sein
he is said to be a good pianist

sondern but. 'Sondern' is a CONJUNCTION that has no effect on the word order of the sentence. It is only used when there is a 'nicht' in the first part of the sentence, and the second part of the sentence contrasts with the first:

sie wohnt nicht in München, sondern in Bonn she lives in Bonn, not in Munich

ss, ß 'ß' is normally used instead of 'ss' in the following circumstances:
1. at the end of a word:
   ich muß I must
   vergiß nicht don't forget
2. before another consonant:
   gemußt had to
   unvergeßlich unforgettable
3. after a long vowel:
   in dem Maße to such an extent
   meine Füße my feet

'ss' is never replaced by 'ß':
1. between vowels when the first vowel is short:
   müssen must
   die Flüsse Europas the rivers of Europe
2. when a word is written in capital letters.

statt takes the genitive. See PREPOSITIONS.

subject case See NOMINATIVE.

subjunctive ◆I *Formation*
1. Present subjunctive

For weak verbs, the present subjunctive only differs from the ordinary present tense in the third person singular, which ends in **-e** instead of **-t**:

ich	sage	*wir*	sagen
du	sagst	*ihr*	sagt
er, sie,		*Sie*	sagen
es	sage	*sie*	sagen

The present subjunctive of strong verbs and modal verbs is formed by adding the following endings to the VERB STEM:

ich	-e	nehme	könne
du	-est	nehmest	könnest
er, sie, es	-e	nehme	könne
wir	-en	nehmen	können
ihr	-et	nehmet	könnet
Sie	-en	nehmen	können
sie	-en	nehmen	können

See also HABEN, SEIN and WERDEN.

....

2. Imperfect subjunctive

The imperfect subjunctive of weak verbs is exactly the same as the ordinary imperfect tense. The imperfect subjunctive of strong verbs is formed by changing any **-a-, -o-,** or **-u-** in the form used for the first person of the ordinary imperfect tense to **-ä-, -ö-,** or **-ü-,** and adding the following endings:

ich	-e	käme	ginge
du	-(e)st	kämest	gingest
er, sie, es	-e	käme	ginge
wir	-en	kämen	gingen
ihr	-(e)t	kämet	ginget
Sie	-en	kämen	gingen
sie	-en	kämen	gingen

The imperfect subjunctive of the modal verbs is the same as the ordinary imperfect tense except that 'dürfen', 'können', 'mögen', and 'müssen' all have an umlaut throughout the imperfect subjunctive:

ich	könnte	*wir*	könnten
du	könntest	*ihr*	könntet
er, sie,		*Sie*	könnten
es	könnte	*sie*	könnten

See also HABEN, SEIN and WERDEN.

3. The perfect subjunctive is formed by using the present subjunctive of 'haben' or 'sein' (whichever is the usual auxiliary) plus the past participle:

sie habe geschlafen
er sei gekommen

4. The pluperfect subjunctive is formed by using the imperfect subjunctive of 'haben' or 'sein' (whichever is the usual auxiliary) plus the past participle:

sie hätte geschlafen
er wäre gekommen

5. The future subjunctive is formed by using the present subjunctive of 'werden' plus the infinitive:

er werde gehen

◆II *Uses of the subjunctive*
   1. In INDIRECT SPEECH:
      **er sagte mir, du wär(e)st nicht dahin-
         gegangen** he told me you hadn't gone
         there
   2. After 'wenn' when the speaker is just
supposing what would happen in a hypothetical
situation:
      wenn er kommen würde *or* **wenn er käme**
         if he were to come
      wenn ich nur reich wäre
         if only I was (*or* were) rich
   3. As an equivalent of 'would' in English,
especially to express wishes, to express the
conditional, and in polite requests:
      das würde ich sehr gerne machen
         I would love to do that
      ich ginge mit, wenn ich Zeit hätte
         I'd go too if I had time
      würden Sie bitte das Fenster zumachen?
         would you shut the window, please?
   4. As an equivalent of 'could' in English,
especially in suggestions and polite requests:
      wir könnten ja ins Kino gehen
         we could always go to the cinema
      könnten Sie mir vielleicht sagen, ...?
         could you possibly tell me ...?

subordinate clauses   A subordinate
clause is a section of a sentence that contains a
subject and a verb but that cannot stand on its
own as a complete sentence. In German,
subordinate clauses have their verb right at the
end of the clause, and the clause is separated off
from the rest of the sentence by commas:
      ich weiß nicht, ob er das machen wollte
         I don't know whether he wanted to do it
      **die Frau, die mir gegenüber saß, war
         wohl eine Schwedin** the woman who was
         sitting opposite me was probably Swedish

....

time The way of telling the time in German is
rather different from English in some ways:
> **zehn (Minuten) vor/nach zehn**
>> ten to/past ten
>
> **Viertel vor zehn, dreiviertel zehn**
>> a quarter to ten
>
> **Viertel nach zehn, viertel elf**
>> a quarter past ten
>
> **halb zehn** half past nine

In connection with time, 'ein' is not declined:
> **um ein Uhr** (*or* **um eins**) at one o'clock

General expressions of time are in the
accusative if there is no preposition:
> **wir sehen uns jeden Dienstag**
>> we see each other every Tuesday

über takes either the accusative or the dative,
depending on whether it is expressing movement
or not. See PREPOSITIONS.

über- is both a SEPARABLE PREFIX and an
INSEPARABLE PREFIX which usually has the
meaning 'over'. If, when it is pronounced, the
main stress falls on 'über-', then the combination
is separable and if the main stress falls on the
actual verb, then it is inseparable:
> **überholen** (*insep*): **er hat den Mercedes
> überholt** he overtook the Mercedes
>
> **überlaufen** (*sep*): **das Wasser ist
> übergelaufen** the water has overflowed

übers a one-word contraction of 'über das'. It
very often replaces the full form, except when 'das'
means 'that particular . . .'. See AM for example.

um 1. As a PREPOSITION, 'um' takes the
accusative.
  2. 'Um . . . zu'. See INFINITIVES II.

um- is both a SEPARABLE PREFIX and
occasionally an INSEPARABLE PREFIX which usually
either means 'around', or has the sense of
changing or redoing something. If the main stress

falls on 'um-', then the combination is separable: if
the main stress falls on the actual verb, then it is
inseparable:

> **umbuchen** (*sep*): **ich hatte auf Dienstag
> umgebucht**
> I'd changed my reservation to Tuesday
> **umarmen** (*insep*): **er umarmte sie**
> he embraced her

ums   is a one-word contraction of 'um das'. It
usually replaces the full form except where 'das'
means 'that particular . . .'. See AM for example.

uns   accusative and dative of 'wir'. See
PERSONAL PRONOUNS.

unser, uns(e)re, unser   our. See
POSSESSIVES.

unter   takes either the accusative or the
dative, depending on whether it is expressing
movement or not. See PREPOSITIONS.

unter-   is both a SEPARABLE PREFIX and an
INSEPARABLE PREFIX which often has the meaning
'under' or 'down'. If the main stress falls on
'unter-', then the combination is separable; if the
main stress falls on the verb itself, then it is
inseparable:

> **unterbrechen** (*insep*): **Entschuldigung,
> ich habe Sie unterbrochen** I'm sorry, I
> interrupted you
> **unterkommen** (*sep*): **sie ist bei
> Verwandten untergekommen**
> she's been put up by relatives

used to   is generally expressed in German by
früher and the perfect tense:

> **früher habe ich Golf gespielt**
> I used to play golf

It is possible to use the imperfect tense of
pflegen instead, but this is rather formal:

> **wie er zu sagen pflegte** as he used to say

....

ver- an INSEPARABLE PREFIX which often has the meaning 'away' or 'wrongly':

> **verreisen: Herr Gipper ist geschäftlich verreist** Herr Gipper is away on business
> **verschlucken: ich habe mich verschluckt** I swallowed the wrong way

verbs There are three types of verb in German – weak, strong, and mixed. Weak verbs are completely regular; strong and mixed verbs are irregular. The 'principle parts' of verbs are – after the infinitive – the 3rd person singular present tense (= he does), the 3rd person singular imperfect tense (= he did), and the past participle (= done). All the other parts and tenses of the verb are formed either from these or from the VERB STEM.

◆I *Weak verbs*

The majority of German verbs are weak. Their principle parts have the following pattern:

spielen	*play*	spielt	spielte	gespielt
lächeln	*laugh*	lächelt	lächelte	gelächelt

But there are a few minor variations:

1. Verbs whose infinitive ends in **-ten, -den, -chnen, -cknen, -dnen, -fnen, -gnen** or **-tmen** add an **-e-** before the **-t** of the last three principle parts:

warten	*wait*	wartet	wartete	gewartet
rechnen	*count*	rechnet	rechnete	gerechnet
regnen	*rain*	regnet	regnete	geregnet
atmen	*breathe*	atmet	atmete	geatmet

2. Verbs whose infinitive ends in **-ieren** or **-eien**, and verbs which start with an INSEPARABLE PREFIX do not add **ge-** at the beginning of the past participle:

studieren	*study*	studiert	studierte	studiert
beruhigen	*calm*	beruhigt	beruhigte	beruhigt
verletzen	*injure*	verletzt	verletzte	verletzt

3. Verbs which start with a SEPARABLE PREFIX add **-ge-** before the stem but after the prefix in the past participle:

| aufwecken *wake up* | weckt auf/ aufweckt | weckte auf/ aufweckte | aufge- weckt |
| vorstellen *introduce* | stellt vor/ vorstellt | stellte vor/ vorstellte | vorge- stellt |

See also SEPARABLE PREFIXES.

◆IIa *Strong verbs*
There are two distinctive characteristics of strong verbs:
1. the vowel in the verb stem is not the same in all the principle parts;
2. the past participle ends in -en:

| sprechen *speak* | spricht | sprach | gesprochen |
| laufen *run* | läuft | lief | gelaufen |

See also IRREGULAR VERBS.

◆IIb *Mixed verbs*
These are a small group of verbs which in one way resemble strong verbs and in another weak verbs:
1. the vowel in the verb stem is not the same in all the principle parts:
2. the past participle ends in -t:

| nennen *call* | nennt | nannte | genannt |
| wissen *know* | weiß | wußte | gewußt |

See also IRREGULAR VERBS.

◆III *The formation of tenses*
There are two types of tense in German – simple and compound. The simple tenses are formed by adding certain endings to the verb stem; the compound tenses are formed by using an AUXILIARY VERB with either the past participle or the infinitive.
The following tables show the formation of all the tenses for weak, strong, and mixed verbs.

Weak verbs

	spielen *play*	**lächeln** *smile*	**warten** *wait*
present participle	spielend	lächelnd	wartend
past participle	gespielt	gelächelt	gewartet

....

imperative

('du' form)	spiel	läch(e)le	wart(e)
('ihr' form)	spielt	lächelt	wartet
('Sie' form)	spielen	lächeln	warten
	Sie	Sie	Sie

present

ich	spiele	läch(e)le	warte
du	spielst	lächelst	wartest
er, sie, es	spielt	lächelt	wartet
wir	spielen	lächeln	warten
ihr	spielt	lächelt	wartet
Sie	spielen	lächeln	warten
sie	spielen	lächeln	warten

imperfect

ich	spielte	lächelte	wartete
du	spieltest	lächeltest	wartetest
er, sie, es	spielte	lächelte	wartete
wir	spielten	lächelten	warteten
ihr	spieltet	lächeltet	wartetet
Sie	spielten	lächelten	warteten
sie	spielten	lächelten	warteten

perfect

ich	habe	habe	habe
	gespielt	gelächelt	gewartet

pluperfect

ich	hatte	hatte	hatte
	gespielt	gelächelt	gewartet

future

ich	werde	werde	werde
	spielen	lächeln	warten

future perfect

ich	werde	werde	werde
	gespielt	gelächelt	gewartet
	haben	haben	haben

conditional

ich	würde	würde	würde
	spielen	lächeln	warten

conditional perfect

ich	würde gespielt haben	würde gelächelt haben	würde gewartet haben

Strong and mixed verbs

	strong **halten** *hold*	mixed **kennen** *know*	+sein **kommen** *come*
present			
participle	haltend	kennend	kommend
past			
participle	gehalten	gekannt	gekommen
imperative			
('du' form)	halt(e)	kenn(e)	komm
('ihr' form)	haltet	kennt	kommt
('Sie' form)	halten Sie	kennen Sie	kommen Sie

present

ich	halte	kenne	komme
du	hältst	kennst	kommst
er, sie, es	hält	kennt	kommt
wir	halten	kennen	kommen
ihr	haltet	kennt	kommt
Sie	halten	kennen	kommen
sie	halten	kennen	kommen

imperfect

ich	hielt	kannte	kam
du	hieltest	kanntest	kamst
er, sie, es	hielt	kannte	kam
wir	hielten	kannten	kamen
ihr	hieltet	kanntet	kamt
Sie	hielten	kannten	kamen
sie	hielten	kannten	kamen

perfect

ich	habe gehalten	habe gekannt	bin gekommen

pluperfect

ich	hatte gehalten	hatte gekannt	war gekommen

....

	future		
ich	werde	werde	werde
	halten	kennen	kommen

	future perfect		
ich	werde	werde	werde
	gehalten	gekannt	gekommen
	haben	haben	sein

	conditional		
ich	würde	würde	würde
	halten	kennen	kommen

	conditional perfect		
ich	würde	würde	würde
	gehalten	gekannt	gekommen
	haben	haben	sein

Information about how the various tenses are used is given in the entries PRESENT TENSE, IMPERFECT TENSE etc. See also WORD ORDER.

verb stem The verb stem is the infinitive minus the **-en** or **-n** at the end:

spiel-en play   **atm-en** breathe
lächel-n smile   **kicher-n** giggle

viel in the singular generally takes no endings unless it is used with a DEMONSTRATIVE or a POSSESSIVE. With the former it will then take the weak ADJECTIVE endings and with the latter the mixed adjective endings:

viel Vergnügen!
    have a good time!
mit viel Mühe
    with a lot of effort
viele Engländer
    a lot of English people
sein vieles Geld
    all his money
mit seinem vielen Geld
    with all the money he has
but note: **vielen Dank!**
    thank you very much

Any adjective coming between 'viel' and the noun when there is no article usually has the strong adjective endings:

mit viel kaltem Wasser
with a lot of cold water

bei viel klassischer Musik
in a lot of classical music

viele ausländische Studenten
a lot of foreign students

'Viel' can be followed by an adjective used as a noun. The adjective is written with a capital letter and has the strong neuter adjective endings:

sie hat viel Gutes getan
she's done a lot of good work

vom is a one-word contraction of 'von dem'. It usually replaces the full form except where 'dem' means 'that particular . . .'. See AM for example.

von takes the dative. Apart from its use as a PREPOSITION, it is used to introduce the person who carries out an action in a PASSIVE sentence.

vor takes either the accusative or the dative, depending on whether it is expressing movement or not. See PREPOSITIONS.

vor- a SEPARABLE PREFIX which very often has the meaning 'in front of someone':

vorführen: der Angeklagte wurde dem Richter vorgeführt the accused was brought before the judge

'Vor-' + adverb combinations can also be used as SEPARABLE PREFIXES:

vorangehen: geh du voran!
you lead the way

vors a one-word contraction of 'vor das'. It often replaces the full form except where 'das' means 'that particular . . .'. See AM for example.

während takes the genitive. See PREPOSITIONS.

....

was 1. an INTERROGATIVE WORD meaning 'what', and a RELATIVE PRONOUN meaning 'that'.

nom	was
acc	was
gen	wessen, (*old*) wes

was hat sie gesagt?
what did she say?

alles, was sie sagte
everything (that) she said

It is very rare nowadays to use 'was' in the dative; the combination 'preposition + was' has been more or less replaced by 'wo- + preposition' written as one word.

2. 'Was' is often used as a short form of ETWAS, especially in spoken and informal German:

ich habe dir was mitgebracht
I've brought something for you

3. The phrase **was für ein** is used like an INTERROGATIVE WORD. The 'was' never changes its form, but 'ein' has its usual endings. When 'was für ein' is used as an article (that is, instead of 'a' or 'the' in front of a noun), the plural form is simply 'was für', but when it is used as a pronoun the plural is 'was für welche':

was für ein Mann ist er?
what sort of man is he?

was für Bücher lesen Sie gern(e)?
what sort of books do you like reading?

was für welche hätten Sie gern(e)?
what sort would you like?

weder is used mainly in the construction **weder ... noch** meaning 'neither ... nor':

sie hat weder angerufen noch geschrieben she neither phoned nor wrote

sie hat weder angerufen, noch hat sie geschrieben she didn't phone, nor did she write

weg away. 'Weg' is used mainly with 'sein' or in phrases without a verb (if there is a verb other

....

than 'sein', the prefix **weg-** is generally used instead):

> **er ist schon weg** he's already gone
> **weg damit!** take it away!

weg- a SEPARABLE PREFIX which usually has the meaning 'away':

> **wegbekommen: ich bekomme den Fleck nicht weg** I can't get rid of this stain

wegen is a PREPOSITION that strictly speaking takes the genitive, but it is much more common nowadays to use the dative, especially in informal and spoken German.

weil because. 'Weil' is a CONJUNCTION that affects the word order of the sentence.

weiter more, else:

> **weiter nichts?** *or* **nichts weiter?** is that all?, nothing else?

weiter- a SEPARABLE PREFIX meaning either 'keep on, carry on' or 'further, on':

> **weiterbestehen: und trotzdem bestehen solche Ungerechtigkeiten weiter** and yet injustices like that still persist
> **weitersagen: sag es aber nicht weiter!** but don't tell anyone else!

welcher, welche, welches has three main functions, but its declension is always the same and an adjective coming after it is always declined with the weak ADJECTIVE endings:

	sing			*pl*
	masc	fem	neut	all genders
nom	welcher	welche	welches	welche
acc	welchen	welche	welches	welche
gen	welches	welcher	welches	welcher
dat	welchem	welcher	welchem	welchen

The only exception is when it is used in exclamations to mean 'what a' or 'what'. In this case it has no ending at all; it may be followed by the indefinite article EIN; and an adjective coming after it is declined with the strong adjective endings:

welch ein Zufall!
what a coincidence!
welch schlechtes Wetter!
what terrible weather!

The three main functions of 'welcher' are:
1. INTERROGATIVE WORD;
2. RELATIVE PRONOUN;
3. INDEFINITE PRONOUN (= 'some' or 'any'). When it is used in this way it has the same number and gender as the noun it refers back to, but its case depends on the function it has in its own sentence or clause:

magst du die? dann nimm dir ruhig welche! do you like these? help yourself to some then
es gibt welche, die das nicht glauben
there are some people who don't believe it

wenig in the singular generally takes no endings unless it is used with a DEMONSTRATIVE or a POSSESSIVE. With the former it will then take the weak ADJECTIVE endings and with the latter the mixed adjective endings:

ich habe nur wenig Geld
I don't have much money
mit wenig Mühe
with little effort
nur wenige Leute
only a few people
von dem wenigen Geld, das wir haben
of the little money we have

Any adjective coming between 'wenig' and the noun after it when there is no article usually has the strong adjective endings:

mit wenig heißem Wasser
with a little hot water
wenige ehemalige Mitglieder
few former members

wenn 1. if. 'Wenn' is a CONJUNCTION that affects the word order of the sentence. It is followed by the SUBJUNCTIVE when the speaker is just supposing what would happen in a situation that seems unlikely to arise, but otherwise it is followed by an ordinary verb:

> **wenn er kommt**
> > if he comes
> **wenn er kommen würde**
> > if he were to come

2. 'Wenn' can also be used to mean WHEN.

wer is both an INTERROGATIVE WORD and a RELATIVE PRONOUN meaning 'who'.

nom	wer
acc	wen
gen	wessen, (*old*) wes
dat	wem

> **wer hat denn das gemacht?**
> > who did that then?
> **wen meinen Sie?**
> > who do you mean?
> **wem haben Sie es gegeben?**
> > who did you give it to?

werden 1. 'Werden' is one of the AUXILIARY VERBS, and it can also be used as the main verb in the sentence (meaning 'to become'), followed either by an adjective or by a noun in the nominative. Its principle parts are:

> werden, wird, wurde, geworden

and it uses 'sein' as its auxiliary.

	present tense	*present subjunctive*
ich	werde	werde
du	wirst	werdest
er, sie, es	wird	werde
wir	werden	werden
ihr	werdet	werdet
Sie	werden	werden
sie	werden	werden

	imperfect tense	*imperfect subjunctive*
ich	wurde	würde
du	wurdest	würdest
er, sie, es	wurde	würde
wir	wurden	würden
ihr	wurdet	würdet
Sie	wurden	würden
sie	wurden	würden

perfect tense
  ich bin geworden *etc*
imperative
  (*'du' form*)   werd(e)
  (*'ihr' form*)   werdet
  (*'Sie' form*)   werden Sie

2. 'Werden' is also used to form the PASSIVE. Its forms are the same as given above with the exception of the perfect and pluperfect passive where 'worden' replaces 'geworden':

   wann ist das Haus gebaut worden?
   when was the house built?

when 1. As a CONJUNCTION, 'when' is translated by **als** when it refers to a single occasion in the past:

   als er nach Hause fuhr, wurde er von der Polizei angehalten when he was driving home he was stopped by the police

When it refers to the present or the future it is translated by **wenn**:

   wenn ich fertig bin, kannst du gehen you can go when I've finished

When it means 'whenever' it is translated by **immer wenn** or **jedesmal wenn**:

   immer wenn ich ihn treffe/traf whenever I meet/met him

2. As an INTERROGATIVE WORD, 'when' is translated by **wann**:

   wann kommt er? when is he coming?
   es ist mir egal, wann er kommt I don't mind when he comes

wie 1. an INTERROGATIVE WORD meaning 'how'.
'Wie' can be combined with certain other words to
produce one-word combinations:
 wieviel how much
 wieso why, how come
2. like, as:
 er war wie ein Bruder zu mir
 he was like a brother to me
See also COMPARISONS III.

wieder- is both a SEPARABLE PREFIX and
occasionally an INSEPARABLE PREFIX which usually
means 're-' or 'again'. If the main stress falls on
'wieder-', then the combination is separable; if the
main stress falls on the actual verb, then it is
inseparable:
 wiedererkennen (*sep*): **die Stadt war nicht
 wiederzuerkennen** the town was
 unrecognizable
 wiederholen (*insep*): **sie wiederholte ihre
 Frage** she repeated her question

wir we. See PERSONAL PRONOUNS.

wo 1. an INTERROGATIVE WORD meaning 'where'.
2. a RELATIVE PRONOUN meaning 'where' or
'when':
 da, wo ich wohne where I live
 damals, wo alle daran glaubten
 in the days when everyone believed in that

wo- is a special form of INTERROGATIVE WORD or
RELATIVE PRONOUN which combines with
prepositions. It is the equivalent of
'was + preposition'. If the preposition begins with
a vowel, the form **wor-** is used instead of **wo-**:
 woher kommt das?
 where does that come from?
 das, worauf sie sich so freute the thing she
 was so looking forward to so much
 worum handelt es sich?
 what's it about?

....

wohl is used as a 'filler word':
    es wird wohl schon zu spät sein
      it'll probably be too late now
    das kann doch wohl nicht wahr sein
      surely that can't be right
    das mag wohl der Fall sein
      that may well be the case

wollen is a MODAL VERB meaning 'want (to)'.
Its principle parts are:
    wollen, will, wollte, gewollt/wollen
and it uses 'haben' as its auxiliary. The present
tense is irregular:

ich	will	*wir*	wollen
du	willst	*ihr*	wollt
er, sie,		*Sie*	wollen
se	will	*sie*	wollen

word division   See HYPHENATION.

word order ◆I *Simple sentences*
    1. The basic word order for a simple sentence is:
    subject – verb – rest of sentence
    ich fahre jeden Tag mit dem Bus
      I go by bus every day
When there is an AUXILIARY VERB and an
infinitive or past participle, the verb slot is filled
by the auxiliary and the other part goes to the end
of the sentence:
    ich bin mit dem Bus gefahren
      I went by bus
If you want to stress a particular part of the rest
of the sentence, you can move it to the front and
put the subject after the verb:
    jeden Tag fahre ich mit dem Bus
      every day I go by bus
    jeden Tag bin ich mit dem Bus gefahren
      every day I went by bus
    2. The word order for a yes-no question is:
    verb – subject – rest of sentence
    fährst du mit dem Bus?
      are you going by bus?

The word order for a question using an
INTERROGATIVE WORD is:
>   question word – verb – (subject) – rest of
sentence
>   **wie lange arbeiten Sie schon hier?**
>   how long have you been working here?
>   **wie lange haben Sie daran gearbeitet?**
>   how long have you been working on it?
>   **wer hat das gesagt?** who said that?

The word order in sentences with separable
verbs is covered under SEPARABLE PREFIXES.

◆II *Subordinate clauses*

Subordinate clauses usually start with a
CONJUNCTION or RELATIVE PRONOUN. They are
separated off from the rest of the sentence by
commas. The basic word order is:
>   conjunction/relative pronoun – subject – rest of
>   sentence – verb:
>   **weil ich mit dem Bus fahre**
>   because I go by bus

When there is an auxiliary verb, it takes over
the verb slot, and the infinitive or past participle
comes just before it:
>   **weil ich mit dem Bus gefahren bin**
>   because I went by bus
>   **er sagte, daß er nicht mitkommen wollte**
>   he said (that) he didn't want to come

When there is an auxiliary and a MODAL VERB
and an infinitive of another verb as well, the
infinitive and the modal verb are put right at the
very end of the clause, after the auxiliary:
>   **wenn ich doch nur mit ihr hätte reden**
>   **können** if only I'd been able to talk to her

Indirect speech is sometimes reported without
the use of 'daß'. When 'daß' is omitted, the word
order is the same as for a simple sentence:
>   **er sagte, er wollte nicht mitkommen**
>   he said he didn't want to come

For the word order in subordinate clauses with
separable verbs see SEPARABLE PREFIXES.

◆III *Complex sentences*

1. Two simple sentences can be joined by **und, oder, aber, sondern, denn,** or **beziehungsweise,** without affecting the word order at all:

> **sie las eine Zeitung, und ich sah fern**
> she read a paper and I watched TV
> **bleibst du zu Hause oder willst du mitkommen?** are you staying at home or do you want to come?

2. A subordinate clause starting with a CONJUNCTION or INTERROGATIVE WORD can simply be added to the end of the main clause:

> **er wußte nicht, wie man das macht**
> he didn't know how that's done
> **ich mußte warten, weil sie ihre Schlüssel vergessen hatte** I had to wait because she'd forgotten her keys

3. A RELATIVE CLAUSE usually comes immediately after the noun that it refers to. But if this would leave an infinitive or past participle completely on its own after the relative clause, it is moved up:

> **wo hast du den Mann, mit dem du gerade gesprochen hast, kennengelernt?**
> where did you meet the man you've just been talking to?

This sentence is possible. But the following form is generally preferred:

> **wo hast du den Mann kennengelernt, mit dem du gerade gesprochen hast?**

4. A subordinate clause starting with a conjunction of time may be put in front of the main clause. If it is, the subject and verb in the main clause are inverted:

> **seit sie verheiratet ist, hat sie sich verändert** she's changed since she got married
> **als sie hereinkam, standen alle auf**
> everyone stood up when she came in

◆IV *Other parts of the sentence*
  1. Expressions of **time, manner** and **place**
come in that order:
> **sie fährt jeden Tag mit ihrem Mann in die
> Stadt** she goes into town every day with
> her husband

  2. The rules for the order of the **object** and
indirect object are:

two nouns:	either order*
two pronouns:	accusative – dative
one noun, one pronoun:	pronoun – noun

> **ich habe es ihm gegeben**
> I gave it to him
> **ich habe es meinem Vater gegeben**
> I gave it to my father
> **ich habe ihm das Buch gegeben**
> I gave him the book

*although it is regarded as strictly correct to put
the indirect object first.

  3. See the entry NEGATIVES for the position of
nicht in the word order.

you has three translations in German – **du,
ihr,** and **Sie.** The difference between them is
explained in the entry PERSONAL PRONOUNS.

zer- an INSEPARABLE PREFIX which has the
general meaning of taking something apart,
destroying it, or getting rid of it:
> **zerbrechen: die Vase ist zerbrochen**
> the vase smashed

zu takes the dative. Apart from its use as an
ordinary PREPOSITION, 'zu' is often used with the
INFINITIVE.

zu- a SEPARABLE PREFIX often meaning
'to(wards)' or having the sense of 'closing':
> **er kam auf mich zu**
> he came towards me
> **er machte die Tür zu**
> he closed the door

zum a one-word contraction of 'zu dem'. It usually replaces the full form except when 'dem' means 'that particular ...'. See AM for example. It is always used instead of the full form when followed by an infinitive used as a noun:

> **es war zum Weinen**
>> it was enough to make you want to cry
> See INFINITIVE III for more examples.

zur a one-word contraction of 'zu der'. It usually replaces the full form except where 'der' means 'that particular ...'. See AM for example.

zurück- a SEPARABLE PREFIX meaning 'back':
> **zurückfinden: finden Sie alleine zurück?**
>> will you be able to find your own way back?

zusammen- a SEPARABLE PREFIX meaning 'together':
> **zusammensetzen: wir setzen uns von Zeit zu Zeit mal zusammen** we get together from time to time

zwischen takes either the accusative or the dative, depending on whether it is expressing movement or not. See PREPOSITIONS.

zwischen- is a prefix used mainly with nouns, but also with a few adjectives and adverbs, with the meaning 'between, intermediate':
> **eine Zwischenmahlzeit**
>> a snack between meals
> **eine Zwischenlösung**
>> an interim solution
> **zwischendurch**
>> in between times

It is very occasionally used as a SEPARABLE PREFIX with verbs, but more often 'dazwischen-' is used instead:
> **zwischenlanden: wir sind in Bahrain zwischengelandet** we made a stopover in Bahrain